IMAGES
of America

FRED HARVEY
HOUSES
OF THE SOUTHWEST

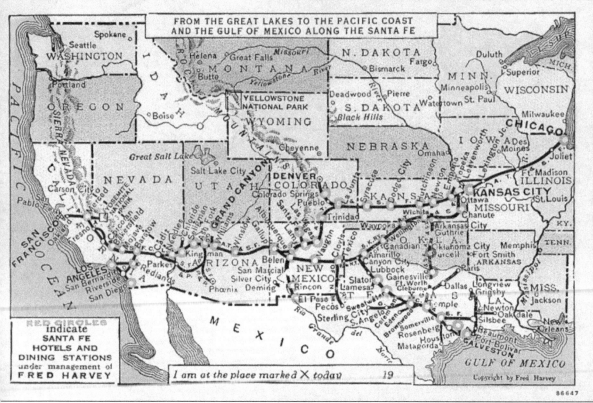

FROM THE GREAT LAKES TO THE PACIFIC COAST
AND THE GULF OF MEXICO ALONG THE SANTA FE

RED CIRCLES indicate
SANTA FE
HOTELS AND
DINING STATIONS
under management of
FRED HARVEY

I am at the place marked X today   19

Copyright by Fred Harvey

86647

HARVEY HOUSE MAP, POSTMARKED 1932. This convenient postcard showed the locations of Harvey services "from the Great Lakes to the Pacific Coast and the Gulf of Mexico along the Santa Fe [Railway]." A tourist need only place an "X" at the Harvey House where he stayed each night or ate each meal, suggesting that a person could enjoy Harvey House hospitality and safety every day of a railroad journey through the Southwest. An eastbound traveler sent this particular postcard home from Needles, California, writing, "Stopped here for half hour for breakfast. Watch this map and you can follow me to Kansas City and Chicago. Don't worry. Nellie." (Author's Fred Harvey collection.)

ON THE COVER: **ALVARADO'S HOTEL.** Tourists examine Native American wares at the entrance to the Indian Arts Building, Alvarado Hotel, Albuquerque, New Mexico, around 1915. (Author's Fred Harvey collection.)

IMAGES
of America

FRED HARVEY
HOUSES
OF THE SOUTHWEST

Richard Melzer

Arizona Historical Foundation

ARCADIA
PUBLISHING

Published by Arcadia Publishing
Charleston, South Carolina

Library of Congress Catalog Card Number: 2007941882

For all general information contact Arcadia Publishing at:
Telephone 843-853-2070
Fax 843-853-0044
E-mail sales@arcadiapublishing.com
For customer service and orders:
Toll-Free 1-888-313-2665

Visit us on the Internet at www.arcadiapublishing.com

*To the dedicated docents at the Harvey House Museum in
Belen, New Mexico.*

CONTENTS

Acknowledgments   6

Introduction   7

1.   Fred Harvey: His Loyal Staff and Legacy   9

2.   Entry to the Southwest: Harvey Houses of Southern Colorado
     and Northeastern New Mexico   25

3.   Las Vegas, New Mexico: The Montezuma and La Castañeda   31

4.   North Central New Mexico: Lamy's El Ortiz and Santa Fe's
     La Fonda   41

5.   Albuquerque: The Alvarado Hotel   51

6.   Scattered Gems: Harvey Houses of Central and Southern
     New Mexico   63

7.   Like Indian Beads: Harvey Houses of Arizona and Southern
     California   79

8.   The Grand Canyon: El Tovar Hotel and Bright Angel Lodge   95

9.   Cultural Tourism: The Southwestern Indian Detours   111

10. End of an Era: 1945–1970   117

ACKNOWLEDGMENTS

Many people have assisted in my historical journey to the Harvey Houses of the Southwest. They include local historians Lila Atkins, David L. Cassey, Ken Fletcher, Sylvia Ligocky, Margaret Espinosa McDonald, and Marshall Trimble, as well as railroad historian Vernon J. Glover, who kindly read the entire text with his usual attention to detail and accuracy. Lesley Poling-Kempes was as helpful as the Harvey Girls she wrote of some 20 years ago.

Thanks also to archivists, librarians, and museum directors, including Donald Burge, Kay Ellermann, Pat Foley, Glenn Fye, Linda Gigick, Colleen Hyde, Daniel Kosharek, Judy Marquez, Maurine McMillan, Chris Nicholl, Esther N. Shir, LeAnn Weller, and Thayla Wright.

Current Harvey House owners Marie Eldh and Allan Affeldt were most gracious and generous with their knowledge. Lisa Bertelli at La Fonda was equally cooperative, in the Fred Harvey tradition.

While space does not allow a complete bibliography, five of the best works on the Fred Harvey Company are Victoria Dye's *All Aboard for Santa Fe: Railway Promotion of the Southwest, 1890s to 1930s* (2005); George H. Foster and Peter C. Weiglin's *Harvey House Cookbook: Memories of Dining along the Santa Fe Railroad* (1992); Marta Weigle and Barbara A. Babcock's *The Great Southwest of the Fred Harvey Company and the Santa Fe Railway* (1996); James D. Henderson's *Meals by Fred Harvey* (1969); and Lesley Poling-Kempes's *The Harvey Girls: Women Who Opened the West* (1989).

A special thanks goes to Fred Harvey collectors Paul Nickens, Robert Strein, Nancy Tucker, and, especially, L. A. Reed of Richmond, Virginia.

Finally, thanks to my wife, Rena, who helped in countless ways as yet another book project ran through our lives like the Santa Fe trains we hear in the distance from our peaceful home in New Mexico.

Unless otherwise noted, all images are from the author's Fred Harvey collection.

INTRODUCTION

The Atchison, Topeka, and Santa Fe Railroad faced a major problem in the mid 1870s: the fledgling railroad lacked sufficient dining facilities for passengers traveling on its long routes through the far Southwest. A typical meal in rail-side restaurants consisted of "overdone" beans, soda biscuits (aptly called "sinkers"), and cold coffee made with highly questionable ingredients. Such food and drink were known to cause stomach cramps at best, dyspepsia at worst. Poor sanitation reigned; utensils and dishes were often old and dirty. Passengers searched in vain for good food, adequate service, and reasonable prices in small towns along the Santa Fe line from Chicago to California.

To make matters worse, passengers complained that in some restaurants their food would have just arrived when the train whistle would suddenly blow, signaling that it was already time to depart. Paying for their uneaten meals, travelers were often the victims of unscrupulous restaurant owners in league with train engineers who knew exactly when to blow their whistles, cheating passengers of both their nourishment and their cash.

Dissatisfied with these eating arrangements, passengers returned home vowing never to ride the Santa Fe again. Worse, dissatisfied travelers advised their friends and relatives to avoid the Santa Fe as well. In short, bad food spelled bad publicity and reduced profits for the railroad. The problem had to be addressed.

The Santa Fe solved its food service problem by turning to an English immigrant whose restaurant in Topeka, Kansas, boasted the three things the railroad needed most: good food, good service, and good prices. Starting with a handshake in 1876 and formalized with a contract two years later, the Santa Fe agreed to build eating houses in towns along its tracks if Fred Harvey agreed to manage them.

The new business relationship enjoyed great success. With much exaggeration, meals at Harvey's restaurant in Topeka were said to be so good that they helped cause a population boom in town: satisfied diners refused to travel any further west once they had experienced Harvey's excellent cuisine. To entice travel beyond Topeka, the Santa Fe built 24 Harvey eating houses or hotels in towns as far west as San Bernardino, California, by 1887. In most cases, the Santa Fe built a Harvey House within months after laying its tracks through each mainline community of any size or distinction. The railroad promised patrons consistently superior food service with the slogan, "Meals by Fred Harvey."

Like all new business ventures, the Harvey Company suffered its share of irksome problems. The company closed two eating houses, at Coolidge and Wallace, New Mexico, when their respective railroad communities declined by the end of the 19th century. Elsewhere, males were not always on their best behavior when entering Harvey establishments. In one legendary incident, a group of local cowhands shouted profanities while riding their horses into the Harvey eating house in Las Vegas, New Mexico. Confronting the troublemakers, Fred Harvey declared, "Gentlemen, ladies dine here. No swearing or foul language is permitted. You must leave quietly at once." The shamed cowhands retreated, their horses in tow. Given such incidents, Harvey is said to have "civilized the West," or at least brought proper Eastern manners to certain rough characters and new communities in the West.

Fire also plagued Fred Harvey's eating houses. Nine of his restaurants burned to the ground before World War I; the Harvey House in Barstow, California, burned three times. Even naming Harvey Houses caused consternation. El Tovar, rather than El Tobar (its correct historical spelling), was chosen so the Grand Canyon resort was less likely to be referred to as "to bar" (or saloon), a dangerous notion on the rim of the mile-deep canyon.

Harvey employees caused additional problems. Male waiters often came to work late and hung over. Many fought while on duty. Witnessing such misbehavior at his eating house in Raton, New Mexico, Fred Harvey reportedly fired his entire staff of waiters on the spot in 1883.

As serious as these problems seemed, Harvey solved each one with a combination of hard work, high standards, and innovative thinking. The Harvey Company's greatest business asset was, in fact, its ability to adjust to changing times and modern passenger needs. By the time of Fred Harvey's death in 1901, his business empire had expanded to include 47 restaurants and 15 hotels. Towns took great pride in their local Harvey Houses, frequently claiming that their particular Harvey establishment was the "crown jewel" (or a similar superlative) of the entire Harvey system; the building of a fine, new Harvey House was seen as a sure sign that a town had shed its frontier reputation and was well on its way to permanency, prosperity, and respectability. Collectively, Fred Harvey Houses were often referred to as "gems" or beautiful "Indian beads" strung beside the Santa Fe's tracks. Harvey Houses and their loyal workers became the subjects of legend, poetry, short stories, novels, and, in 1946, a famous motion picture and hit song. The purpose of this book is to describe the remarkable growth and success of 26 Harvey Houses located in a region whose identity was largely shaped and, yes, exploited by the combined efforts of the Fred Harvey Company and the Santa Fe Railway. At the heart of the famous Fred Harvey system, the Southwest, including southern Colorado, New Mexico, Arizona, and parts of southern California, is the focus of the history and images that follow.

But a history of the Harvey Houses in the Southwest is not just the history of a company and its many public buildings, however successful and unique they once were. This story must include the thousands of loyal Harvey workers, as well as the millions of railroad travelers who enjoyed the company's dining and hotel services. Photographs of these workers and guests are in many ways as important and as engaging as are images of the Harvey Houses themselves.

Many of the images in this brief study were originally produced and sold as Fred Harvey postcards, used to advertise the Southwest as a major tourist destination. In conjunction with the Detroit Publishing Company, Fred Harvey was one of the largest postcard manufacturers in the entire country; the company produced 179 images of the Grand Canyon alone. An estimated half million postcards were sold at Harvey House newsstands each year in the early 20th century, a period known as the golden age of postcard popularity in the United States. Although Fred Harvey postcard images of Native Americans were sometimes distorted for commercial purposes, most postcard images of the Harvey Houses and their staffs remain reliable sources of information about a passing era in hospitality in the American Southwest.

One

FRED HARVEY
HIS LOYAL STAFF AND LEGACY

FRED HARVEY. Fred Harvey was born in London, England, on June 27, 1835. At 15, he joined the millions of others who migrated to the United States with little money in their pockets but great ambition in their souls. Starting as a dishwasher in a New York City restaurant, Harvey advanced to progressively better jobs in New Orleans, St. Louis, and Leavenworth, Kansas. While working in rail mail transport, he could not help but notice the poor quality of food and service available to most train passengers. In 1875, Harvey and a partner opened their own rail-side restaurant in Topeka, Kansas, a venture that proved so successful that Harvey proposed to run similar establishments for the Burlington Railroad, which foolishly refused the offer, and to the Atchison, Topeka, and Santa Fe Railroad, which wisely accepted it. Harvey ran his new business enterprise until his death in 1901, when his capable sons, Byron and Ford, took over. Byron S. Harvey Jr. became the Harvey Company's president in 1946. (Courtesy of Marshall Trimble.)

H-2929   PETTICOAT LANE EAST FROM MAIN STREET, KANSAS CITY, MO.

FRED HARVEY NEWSPAPER AD. Fred Harvey originally hired male waiters but found most of them deficient in proper behavior, attire, and most importantly service to customers. After firing the entire male staff at his eating house in Raton, Harvey was inspired to hire only female servers. He soon ran a classified ad in several Midwestern newspapers: "Young women 18 to 30 years of age, of good moral character, attractive and intelligent, to waitress in Harvey Eating Houses on the Santa Fe in the West. Wages, $17.50 per month with room and board. Liberal tips customary. Experience not necessary. Write Fred Harvey, Union Depot, Kansas City, Missouri." Thousands of women responded and were seen by Harvey interviewer Alice Steel at company headquarters in Kansas City. Steel was known to ask many pointed questions and required each applicant to sign a statement attesting to her "good moral character," if such a declaration was in fact true. As Harvey Girl Mary G. Wright later recalled, "I am sure it was never so hard to enlist in the army."

HARVEY GIRLS BESIDE THE HARVEY HOUSE IN BELEN, NEW MEXICO, C. 1931. There were five main reasons why women responded to Fred Harvey's newspaper want ads. First, Harvey Girl applicants sought career opportunities that seldom existed in the rural communities where many had spent their early lives. Other women became Harvey Girls hoping to meet eligible Western males. Making good money in wages and tips, many girls hoped to save for their trousseaus, raise money for their education, create personal nest eggs, or assist their financially strapped families back home. In contrast, some women hoped to escape abusive relationships back home. Finally, as one Harvey Girl later recalled, "So many of us couldn't afford to travel and see the world. We didn't see the world, but we saw the West and parts of the country we would not have otherwise seen." For whatever reason they became Harvey Girls, theirs was a coming of age experience that profoundly shaped the rest of their lives. (Courtesy of the Belen Harvey House Museum.)

HARVEY GIRLS AND STAFF IN ASH FORK AND KINGMAN, ARIZONA, C. 1925. Women were proud to be selected as Harvey Girls, a name they preferred because "waitresses" were often identified as women of ill repute in the West. Who were the Harvey Girls? A sample of 165 Harvey Girls listed in U.S. Census reports from 1900 to 1930 reveals that 55 percent were native to the Midwest, 30 percent came from other parts of the United States, and 15 percent were foreign-born, most often from northern and western Europe. Eighty percent of the Harvey Girls were single, ten percent were married, five percent were widowed, and five percent were divorced. Some were relatives. The average age was 29, with one Harvey Girl as young as 15 and one as old as 58. (Courtesy of Marshall Trimble and the Mohave Museum.)

A HARVEY GIRL AT EL ORTIZ, LAMY, NEW MEXICO, C. 1912. Harvey Girls were normally trained for six weeks before being assigned to their first, usually small, Harvey House. With time and success, many women graduated to larger, busier houses, although some preferred smaller operations for personal reasons, including climate and cultural surroundings. According to a Harvey Girl training manual, these are a few of the many rules young trainees learned: In setting tables, always place forks to the left, knives and spoons to the right; "Sparkling bright" glasses (with no chips or cracks) are placed above the blade of the knife; all food is served from the left; all beverages are served from the right; compliment children, "if possible"; never chat with other Harvey Girls while customers are present; never get into an argument with a guest; "SMILE. Remember that a smile on your face is [an essential] part of the Harvey Girl uniform." (Courtesy of L. A. Reed.)

HARVEY GIRLS AT LA JUNTA, COLORADO'S, EL OTERO LUNCHROOM, 1936. After polling their on-board passengers, railroad personnel wired ahead to the next Harvey House to let the house manager know how many travelers planned to eat when the train stopped for a meal. After years of experience, house managers knew to expect 90 percent of all passengers to stop for breakfast, 40 percent to stop for lunch, and 60 percent to stop for dinner. Engineers blew their train whistles about a mile out of town to alert Harvey House personnel of their impending arrival. A porter struck a gong, placed near Harvey House entrances, to announce when each new group of hungry passengers had arrived. (Courtesy of L. A. Reed.)

HARVEY HOUSE CHECK.

Once passengers were seated, Harvey Girls took drink orders using a "cup code" to indicate what beverage each customer had ordered: when a cup was turned up it meant coffee, down it meant hot tea, and so on. Harvey Girls used similar techniques to serve the balance of each meal as quickly, efficiently, and cordially as possible. Even Harvey House lunch counters were shaped in horseshoe designs to maximize serving efficiency. Led by their "wagon boss," or head waitress, Harvey Girls served each trainload of 60 to 100 travelers (with 16 customers assigned to each Harvey Girl's station) within 30 minutes, the same amount of time needed to change railroad crews and service a train with fuel and water. House managers calmly announced when customers had 10 minutes to finish their meals and reboard their waiting trains. Managers also assured customers that no one would be left behind.

FRED HARVEY

Waitress	No. Served	Amount	
			F916501

BAR

Fred Harvey ®

F916501

Waitress_____

No. Served_____

Table No._____

Item	Amount
	Food
	Bar
	Tax
Please Pay Cashier	Total

F.H. 1183 (9-66)

MADGE PINKERTON AND A KITCHEN WORKER, BELEN HARVEY HOUSE, 1927. All Harvey Girls were required to wear a standard uniform that included black dresses, white aprons, black shoes, black hose, and white ribbons in their hair. Shoes were to be shined and uniforms were to be spotless; the slightest stain required an immediate change of dress. According to Dorothy Bowe, who worked at La Fonda in Santa Fe for eight years, "Each morning we had to pass inspection before going out on the floor. If anything was wrong, you were sent back to your room to correct [it]." Intentionally, Harvey Girl uniforms appeared puritanical, especially compared to the questionable attire of dance hall girls employed in notorious Western saloons. (Courtesy of the Belen Harvey House Museum.)

COLTER HALL (LEFT) AT THE GRAND CANYON, 1956. Unmarried Harvey Girls were required to live in dorms located in or near the Harvey Houses in which they worked. Two girls shared each well-kept bedroom, with a common bathroom down the hall. The Harvey Company hired matrons to chaperon their dorms and strictly enforce Harvey House rules. These rent-free living quarters were economical and convenient for Harvey Girls, who often worked long hours and split shifts. Isolated and protected, the dorms also added a sense of security for newly arrived female employees and their worried families back home. Living and working together, wearing the same uniforms, and proudly maintaining the same high standards helped to create strong personal bonds and an esprit de corps seldom found in workplaces, then or now. (Courtesy of the Grand Canyon National Park Museum Collection, No. 03181.)

GLADYS SNYDER RITCHIE, C. 1928. Gladys Snyder was 18 years old when she went to work as a Harvey Girl at the Harvey House in Clovis, New Mexico. Although company rules forbade it, Gladys soon dated 20-year-old John C. Ritchie, a six-foot-six-inch Harvey House cook. The couple fell in love and married on December 13, 1930. Other Harvey Girls married much sooner, despite signing contracts that specified that they could not marry during their first term of employment. Some say the Harvey Girls married so quickly that marriage proposals for the pretty ones took a day, while proposals for less attractive ones took three, a theory that certainly did not apply to beautiful Gladys Snyder. Thousands of Harvey Girls exchanged their Harvey uniforms for bridal gowns, marrying eligible young cowboys, ranchers, miners, businessmen, and, most often, railroad men. Grateful to Fred Harvey for bringing them together (however unintentionally), former Harvey Girls and their husbands frequently named their first-born son Fred or Harvey or both. (Courtesy of the Belen Harvey House Museum.)

HARVEY GIRLS AND STAFF AT THE BELEN HARVEY HOUSE, c. 1925. When not working long hours, Harvey Girls usually relaxed with fellow employees. Most amusements were quite innocent. In Belen, Ruth Armstrong and her Harvey Girl friends enjoyed walking to the local post office, often stopping at a soda shop on the way home to their Harvey House. More adventuresome girls enjoyed hiking and picnicking. But, like other young people, Harvey Girls occasionally drank too much, danced too wildly, or simply stayed out too late. Getting caught breaking their 10:00 p.m. curfew led to stern warnings by dorm matrons; being caught three times could mean dismissal. Clever Harvey Girls devised methods to enter their dorms without detection. In some Harvey Houses, girls achieved late-night entries by climbing ivy-covered ladders leading to second-floor dorm windows. (Courtesy of the Belen Harvey House Museum.)

THE ALVARADO HOTEL, ALBUQUERQUE, C. 1930. Harvey Girls were the best known employees on a Harvey House staff, but they were only the most visible members of a large, well-coordinated team. Other important team members included managers, chefs, bakers, busboys, dishwashers, and newsstand employees. Harvey hotels and resorts had even larger staffs, including desk clerks, chambermaids, porters, bellboys, curio shop managers, and in larger hotels, barbers. Like the Harvey Girls, many of these male and female employees were young and single. Unlike the Harvey Girls, they sometimes included local Hispanic and Native American residents, albeit usually in the lowest level, most menial jobs. Nevertheless, most employees enjoyed working for Fred Harvey, staying on for several decades and whole careers. (Courtesy of the Albuquerque Museum Photo Collection, No. PA1981.082.001.)

HARVEY HOUSE STAFF, C. 1931. Pictured here from left to right are Chef Barberi and cooks Ramon Saavedra, Joe Taylor, and Joe Tafoya outside the Belen Harvey House. Chefs were particularly important members of each Harvey House staff. The Harvey Company spared no expense in attracting and retaining the best chefs to even the most remote Harvey Houses. Many chefs were European. Konrad Allgaier served as the Kaiser's personal chef in Germany before arriving in the United States in 1922 and working at La Fonda in Santa Fe for many years. Other chefs came from Italy, Denmark, Switzerland, and France; they often trained American chefs who had started as Harvey House cooks and earned promotions from one Harvey House to another, starting in small houses like Belen and culminating at Harvey resorts like El Tovar at the Grand Canyon. Other famous Harvey House chefs included John Frenden (who worked for Fred Harvey for 47 years), Martin Rapp (at La Castañeda in Las Vegas, New Mexico), Charles Zuellig (at the Alvarado in Albuquerque), and James Marques (at El Tovar). (Courtesy of the Belen Harvey House Museum.)

BELEN HARVEY HOUSE MANAGER, HIS WIFE, AND HARVEY GIRLS, C. 1931. According to U.S. Census reports from 1900 to 1930, the average Harvey House manager was 40 years old and married; some were World War I veterans. While many were native-born Americans, over 50 percent were first- or second-generation European immigrants. Like Harvey Girls and chefs, most managers followed career paths by working in smaller Harvey operations and, if successful, gaining promotions to larger, busier houses, culminating in places like the Alvarado in Albuquerque. At least one Harvey Girl, Joanne Stinelichner, was promoted to serve as a manager. Well trained and well paid, Harvey House managers adhered to a single guiding principle: "Maintenance of service regardless of cost." According to one story, a Harvey House manager facing a $1,000 loss attempted to cut corners and turn his loss into a significant profit for the company. When Fred Harvey learned of this cost-cutting scheme, he fired the manager, declaring that high standards were far more important than high profits in serving the traveling public. (Courtesy of the Belen Harvey House Museum.)

TOM OF GANADO, ARIZONA, AND NATIVE AMERICAN QUARTERS, THE ALVARADO HOTEL, C. 1910. Native Americans played key roles on Harvey House staffs. Although not directly employed by Harvey, many Native Americans sold their goods to tourists outside Harvey Houses. Others, like Tom and his wife, Elle, demonstrated artistic skills or performed native dances. A few Native Americans worked in Harvey kitchens and hotels, usually in menial, low-paying jobs; they rarely entered the ranks of management. In short, most Native Americans were employed—some would say exploited—for their ability to help promote Fred Harvey's hotels and restaurants, rather than to provide opportunities for high paying jobs or upward social mobility. So many Navajo and Pueblo Indians worked at Fred Harvey operations at the Alvarado and the Grand Canyon that the company provided them with nearby space on which to build their living quarters.

MARY COLTER (RIGHT) EXAMINING PLANS WITH EL TOVAR MANAGER VICTOR PATROSSO
AND ANNA ICKES, WIFE OF SECRETARY OF THE INTERIOR HAROLD ICKES, AT THE GRAND
CANYON, C. 1935. Starting in 1902 at the Alvarado Hotel in Albuquerque, Mary Colter served
as the architect or chief interior designer for 22 Fred Harvey projects in a career that spanned
nearly half a century. An early success in a male-dominated profession, Colter incorporated local
landscape and culture into Harvey House decor, from Navajo sand paintings at El Navajo in
Gallup, New Mexico, to Spanish santos (religious sculptures) at La Posada in Winslow, Arizona.
Colter even designed Harvey House and Santa Fe Railway dining car china, using patterns from
Mimbres Indian pottery. Colter became famous for her passion for detail and authenticity, often
rejecting plans, artifacts, and even finished work if they did not meet her high standards. (Courtesy
of the Grand Canyon National Park Museum Collection, No. 16941.)

Two

Entry to the Southwest
Harvey Houses of Southern Colorado and Northeastern New Mexico

Santa Fe Depot & Harvey House,   La Junta, Colo.   Moyemont

EL OTERO, LA JUNTA, COLORADO, C. 1914. As the first Harvey House on the Santa Fe Railway in the Southwest, El Otero was named to honor the Miguel A. Otero family, who had played a key role in the development of the railroad and business in southeastern Colorado and much of New Mexico. The Harvey Company named its hotels and restaurants to honor deserving families and individuals, but, most importantly, as a marketing technique to create an exotic theme that might draw tourists eager for new cultural experiences in what anthropologists now call "cultural tourism." Originally a Harvey eatery opened in 1883, El Otero included a 121-seat dining room and 44 hotel rooms (13 of which had private baths) by 1895. (Courtesy of L. A. Reed.)

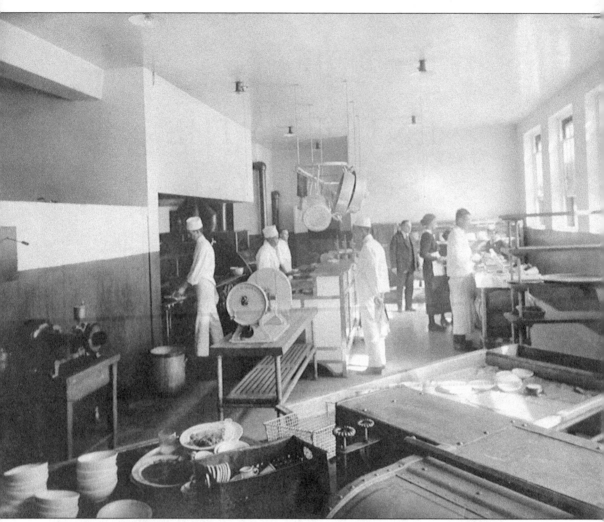

EL OTERO'S KITCHEN, C. 1920. D. K. Spencer was only 15 when he began working at El Otero. Assigned to the storeroom, Spencer worked with large shipments of everything from produce to liquor, the latter kept in a storeroom "locked with access only by the hotel manager." Spencer especially admired a European baker named Ernest Stangl. "We always knew when Stangl was on duty as he raised the great gobs of bread dough over his head and slammed them down on the table, pounding the air out of them. . . . His bakery goods were . . . in such a great demand by all dining cars [on the Santa Fe Railway] that stewards would order enough bakery goods at La Junta to last to Los Angeles and back." (Courtesy of the University of Arizona, Special Collections, AZ326, Box 4, Folder 2.)

HARVEY HOUSE AND LUNCHROOM, COLORADO SPRINGS, COLORADO, C. 1910. The *Colorado Springs Evening Gazette* noted the "handsome addition" of an eating house to the town's existing train depot in 1899. Ably managed by the Harvey Company, the house served a maximum of 48 travelers in its lunchroom and an additional 59 customers in its dining room. (Courtesy of the University of Arizona, Special Collections, AZ326, Box 4, Folder 1.)

SANTA FE RAILWAY DEPOT AND HARVEY HOUSE, TRINIDAD, COLORADO, 1915. Located in a wood-frame building, the Fred Harvey eating house in Trinidad had opened by 1895. A new structure, designed in Mission Revival style architecture, was built at a cost of $38,174.98 (over $900,000 in today's money) and was opened on June 1, 1903. The house was named in honor of Don García López de Cárdenas, Francisco Coronado's *maestre de campo*, or second in command, during the first Spanish exploration of the Southwest from 1540 to 1542. Naming Harvey Houses after Spanish explorers helped tourists feel that they too were explorers of the Southwest and its landscape, history, and cultures. Fred Harvey's son-in-law John F. Huckel was said to have named most of the Harvey Houses in the region. (Courtesy of L. A. Reed.)

THE CARDENAS'S HOTEL LOBBY AND DINING ROOM, C. 1914. The hotel's 25 rooms rented for $3 to $4 per night ($62 to $83 in today's money). Famous guests included renowned orator and three-time presidential candidate William Jennings Bryan. The Cardenas's lunchroom, seating 35 customers, charged 75¢ a meal. The dining room sat 102. (Courtesy of L. A. Reed.)

STAFF AT THE HARVEY EATING ROOM, RATON, NEW MEXICO, 1894. Opened in 1882, Fred Harvey's eating room in Raton was located just north of the town's Santa Fe depot (below). In May 1903, E. M. Clendening of the Commercial Club of Kansas City visited the eatery and, upon returning home, wrote to Harvey headquarters that "every one of your employees, from the young women who waited on the table to the manager, vied with each other in endeavoring to render perfect service." Despite such praise, the Harvey Company closed its eating room in Raton shortly after Mr. Clendening had conveyed his appreciation. With new Harvey Houses in Trinidad to the north and Las Vegas to the south, an eating room in Raton was no longer needed. (Courtesy of the Raton Public Library.)

Three

LAS VEGAS, NEW MEXICO
THE MONTEZUMA
AND LA CASTAÑEDA

MONTEZUMA HOTEL, MONTEZUMA, NEW MEXICO, C. 1882. The Montezuma represented Fred Harvey's first luxury resort hotel. Located northeast of Las Vegas at the end of a 6-mile spur line connected to the Santa Fe's main line, the grand hotel was named for the Aztec ruler Montezuma, who, according to local Native American legend, once lived among the Pueblos of northern New Mexico. Built by Jerome, Rice, Moore, and Emery of Kansas City using popular Queen Ann architecture, the hotel was completed in 1882 at a cost of $300,000 (over $6 million in today's money). With 270 guest rooms, the Montezuma was the largest Fred Harvey resort ever built. At its height, the hotel entertained as many as 18,000 guests per year. (Courtesy of the Museum of New Mexico, Photo Archives, No. 86964.)

MONTEZUMA'S OPENING NIGHT PROGRAM, APRIL 17, 1882. Over 400 guests attended this gala event, featuring a keynote address by Fred Harvey himself. According to the *Las Vegas Daily Optic*, the U.S. Army Band from nearby Fort Union provided music for dancers in a ball that lasted long into the night. (Courtesy of the Las Vegas Museum and Rough Rider Memorial Collection, No. 2005.11.2.)

MONTEZUMA'S GRAND DINING ROOM, C. 1902. Lavishly decorated with eight chandeliers, Montezuma's dining room catered to wealthy tastes in both decor and cuisine. For specialty dishes, the Harvey Company even arranged for 200-pound green turtles to be shipped from northern Mexico and for sea celery to be shipped from the Gulf of Lower California. (Courtesy of the Las Vegas Museum and Rough Rider Memorial Collection.)

THE ∴ ▴ ▴ ▴
MONTEZUMA

Las Vegas Hot Springs,
NEW MEXICO.

The Land of Sunshine.

AN
IDEAL
HEALTH
AND
PLEASURE
RESOR⊤.

. . . This splendid hostelry, which is 7,000 feet above sea level, is open all the year round. No traveler via the Santa Fe route should neglect spending a few days at

...THE MONTEZUMA...

Clark D. Frost,
Manager.

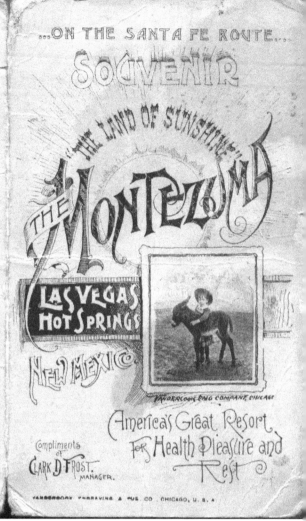

...ON THE SANTA FE ROUTE...

SOUVENIR

"THE LAND OF SUNSHINE"

THE MONTEZUMA

LAS VEGAS HOT SPRINGS

NEW MEXICO

VANDERCOOK ENG COMPANY CHICAGO

America's Great Resort for Health Pleasure and Rest

Compliments of CLARK D. FROST, Manager.

VANDERCOOK ENGRAVING & PUB. CO., CHICAGO, U. S. A.

BROCHURE FOR THE MONTEZUMA HOTEL, C. 1890. With 40 nearby mineral springs, the Montezuma was advertised as a major health resort. Brochures like this one claimed that drinking the water and bathing in local spas could "almost invariably" cure such illnesses as rheumatism, gout, mental exhaustion, "nervous afflictions," spinal disorders, dyspepsia, liver disorders, diabetes, and "female diseases." Guests were also offered "mud baths" to help relieve pain and serve as a soothing counterirritant. According to historian Sandra D. Lynn, "The patient . . . wallowed, piglike, for a time and then emerged from the tub sleek with black mud and ready to be washed and dried." Strange what the rich would do—and pay for—in their quest for better health in the Gilded Age of the late 19th century. (Courtesy of the Las Vegas Museum and Rough Rider Memorial Collection, No. 2005.42.1.)

MONTEZUMA'S HOTEL LOBBY, 1902. An early guest named Charles Dambmann had been sent west by his wealthy parents in an effort to salvage a wasted life filled with wine, women, and cards. Instead, Dambmann caused a national scandal by marrying a Russian diva, spending lavishly in Montezuma's honeymoon suite and conducting high-stakes games of chance in his hotel quarters. (Courtesy of the Las Vegas Museum and Rough Rider Memorial Collection.)

MONTEZUMA, C. 1895. Bellboys wait to greet guests at the entrance to the Montezuma Hotel. (Courtesy of the Las Vegas Museum and Rough Rider Memorial Collection, No. 66.67.1.)

34

A MONTEZUMA GUEST ROOM, 1902. The Montezuma was designed to allow abundant sunlight and fresh mountain air into each of its guest rooms. Famous guests included presidents Ulysses S. Grant and Rutherford B. Hayes and their wives. Given her aversion to liquor, it is certain that "Lemonade Lucy" Hayes consumed only non-alcoholic beverages during her brief respite at the Montezuma. (Courtesy of the Las Vegas Museum and Rough Rider Memorial Collection.)

GUESTS RELAX ON THE MONTEZUMA'S WIDE PORCH, C. 1890. The hotel's extensive grounds included fountains, lush lawns, graveled walks, trees, rare flowers, and a miniature zoo. Athletic guests could enjoy archery, lawn tennis, cricket, croquet, and bowling (on 11 lanes). More adventuresome guests rode saddle horses and burros. (Courtesy of the Las Vegas Museum and Rough Rider Memorial Collection.)

FIREFIGHTERS AT THE MONTEZUMA HOTEL, JANUARY 1884. Although advertised as "absolutely fireproof" when it opened in 1882, the Montezuma was largely consumed by flames in January 1884. Rebuilt, the hotel reopened on April 20, 1885, with new fire prevention systems but suffered yet another disastrous fire less than four months later on August 9, 1885. Rebuilt again, the hotel was renamed The Phoenix, suggesting that it had risen from its own ashes when it opened for a third time on August 16, 1886. Preferring to have potential guests forget its unfortunate history of fires, the hotel soon reverted to its original name. But nothing could save the hotel from economic crises, especially the national depression of the 1890s. Experiencing losses of up to $40,000 a year, the hotel was closed to all but summer guests from September 1, 1893, to October 31, 1903. Permanently closed on the latter date, the Harvey Company sold most of the hotel's elaborate furnishings to the St. Louis World Fair Hotel. (Courtesy of the Museum of New Mexico, Photo Archives, No. 121216.)

H-1854. HOTEL CASTANEDA, LAS VEGAS, NEW MEXICO.

LA CASTAÑEDA HOTEL, LAS VEGAS, NEW MEXICO, C. 1910. Located just east of the Santa Fe Railway depot in Las Vegas, La Castañeda was named for Pedro de Castañeda de Nagera, the chief chronicler of Francisco Coronado's expedition to the Southwest from 1540 to 1542. Replacing a small Harvey lunchroom opened in 1883, La Castañeda was designed by California architects Frederic Louis Roehrig and A. Reinsch using, for the first time in New Mexico, Mission Revival style architecture. The hotel was built at a cost of $110,000 ($2.7 million in today's money) and was furnished with an additional $30,000 (over $730,000 in today's money). Opened on January 1, 1899, La Castañeda represented the first of a new generation of grand Harvey House hotels.

HOTEL CASTANEDA, LAS VEGAS, N. M.

LA CASTAÑEDA, C. 1915. Fashionable young women and others gather by the tracks outside La Castañeda. A favorite pastime in railroad towns like Las Vegas was to wait for passenger trains to see which celebrities might be passing through, stopping for a meal, or, best yet, staying the night. (Courtesy of L. A. Reed and La Castañeda Hotel Historical Collection.)

LA CASTAÑEDA'S 108-SEAT DINING ROOM AND 51-SEAT LUNCHROOM, C. 1910. For passengers not in a hurry to catch trains, Fred Harvey's dining rooms offered luxurious dining, complete with fine Irish linen and expensive English silverware, often bought by Harvey himself on his visits to Europe. The Harvey Company kept a silverware set worth $200,000 at La Castañeda, perhaps left from the Montezuma's collection of expensive silverware after the grand resort had closed in 1903. La Castañeda's staff used this silverware on special occasions under the watchful eye of Bridget Malone, the dining room's lead Harvey Girl for 30 years. When needed for banquets at other Harvey Houses, the silverware was carefully packed, closely guarded in transport by train, and finally returned to safe quarters in La Castañeda. (Courtesy of the University of Arizona, Special Collections, AZ326, Box 8, Folder 3.)

LA CASTAÑEDA'S MAIN LOBBY WITH STAIRS TO GUEST ROOMS, C. 1910. La Castañeda offered patrons 37 guest rooms on the second floor of the hotel. (Courtesy of the University of Arizona, Special Collections, AZ326, Box 8, Folder 3.)

TEDDY ROOSEVELT OUTSIDE LA CASTAÑEDA, 1899. La Castañeda served as the headquarters of the first Rough Riders reunion, a year after the Spanish-American War. The charismatic Roosevelt drew hundreds of admirers when he arrived on June 24, 1899. Roosevelt and many other Rough Riders stayed at La Castañeda, although they reportedly left the new hotel in a "deplorable" state. (Courtesy of the Museum of New Mexico, Photo Archives, No. 14292.)

Four

NORTH CENTRAL NEW MEXICO
LAMY'S EL ORTIZ AND SANTA FE'S LA FONDA

EL ORTIZ, LAMY, NEW MEXICO, 1910. Replacing a Harvey lunchroom opened in 1883, El Ortiz was built in Pueblo Revival style architecture, using plans by Louis Curtiss, with interior designs by Mary Colter. Originally named Los Pinos, the hotel was renamed El Ortiz just prior to its opening in 1910; according to Santa Fe Railway president Edward P. Ripley, El Ortiz was the "more euphonious" of the two names. In either case, the new Harvey House honored prominent Hispanic families that had, in fact, intermarried, becoming the still-influential Ortiz y Pinos. (Courtesy of Nancy Tucker.)

LOBBY, EL ORTIZ, C. 1910. An 18-mile spur line connects the railroad from Lamy to Santa Fe. Passengers who did not travel north for accommodations in Santa Fe could relax at El Ortiz. With 34 seats at its lunch counter, a dozen seats in its dining room, and eight guest rooms in a town of 329 residents (in 1930), El Ortiz was called "the littlest hotel in the littlest town."

GUESTS IN EL ORTIZ'S INTERIOR COURTYARD, C. 1925. After a brief stay in Lamy, Owen Wister (author of *The Virginian*) wrote to the hotel's manager to compare El Ortiz to "a private house of someone who had lavished thought and care upon every nook. . . . The temptation was to give up all plans and stay a week for the pleasure of . . . resting in such a place." (Courtesy of L. A. Reed.)

LA FONDA, C. 1900. This postcard shows La Fonda as it appeared in the 19th century. Previously known as the Exchange Hotel and as the United States Hotel, La Fonda (meaning "The Inn") had served as the main hotel in Santa Fe since as early as the 17th century. With the opening of the Santa Fe Trail in 1821, it became known as "The Inn at the End of the Trail." Historian Ralph Emerson Twitchell described the hotel's *gran bailes* (grand balls) at which guests consumed "case after case" of champagne and danced to the music of fine orchestras, giving Santa Fe "a reputation for hospitality and good cheer unequaled in the great Southwest." Twitchell also described La Fonda's always-crowded gambling room, where guests played "every kind of gambling game known in the West." Even Doña Tules (Gertrudis Barceló), Santa Fe's most famous female gambler, dealt cards at the hotel's gambling tables. Unfortunately, violence sometimes marred La Fonda's tranquility. In 1867, W. L. Rynerson shot and killed Territorial Supreme Court Chief Justice John P. Slough in one of the most famous murder cases in New Mexico history.

LA FONDA UNDERGOING MAJOR REMODELING AND EXPANSION, C. 1928. The old La Fonda was demolished (with the aid of a World War I tank) in April 1919. A rebuilt La Fonda reopened on December 30, 1922. The Santa Fe Railway acquired the property in 1925 and leased it to the Harvey Company the following year. In 1928, the building underwent extensive remodeling and an expansion of 46 rooms and suites under the direction of John Gaw Meem, the most famous Pueblo Revival architect in New Mexico history. Mary Colter designed the hotel's interior with the help of several Santa Fe artists, including Gerald Cassidy, Olive Rush, and Paul Lantz. In her typical fashion, Colter made each guest room unique in colors, decoration, furniture, and fixtures. Asked if she was nervous about decorating a hotel in a city full of world-famous artists, Colter replied, "I'm scared to death." She need not have worried. Once finished, her work was applauded by everyone in town—even the artists. The 156-room hotel reopened on May 18, 1929. (Courtesy of La Fonda History Collection.)

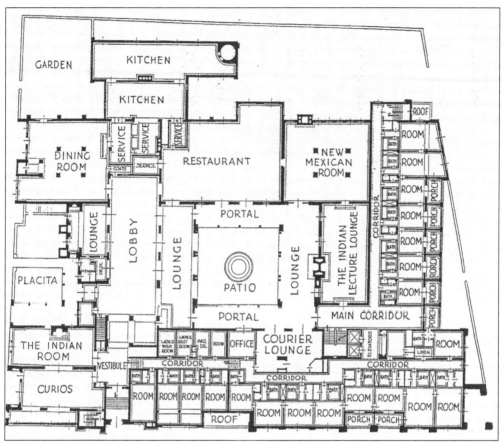

LA FONDA FIRST-STORY FLOOR PLAN BY JOHN GAW MEEM. La Fonda represented Meem's first major commission and, some say, his "master work." (Courtesy of La Fonda History Collection.)

NORTHWEST CORNER OF THE REMODELED LA FONDA, C. 1940. During La Fonda's expansion, the *Santa Fe New Mexican* reported that workers unearthed some interesting artifacts and remains, including a cannon ball, a loaded revolver, many bottles of whiskey, and even a human skull.

LA FONDA'S LOBBY, C. 1930. Journalist Ernie Pyle visited Santa Fe in the 1930s and asserted that "life among the upper crust is centered . . . in the La Fonda Hotel. . . . You could go there any time of day and see a few artists in the bar, or an Indian that some white woman loved, or a goateed nobleman from Austria, or a maharaja from India, or a New York broker, or an archaeologist, or some local light in overalls and cowboy boots. You never met anybody anywhere except at the La Fonda." While Pyle panned this exotic mixture of locals and guests, another newsman thrived on it. For years, *Santa Fe New Mexican* reporter Brian Boru "B. B." Dunne sat in the same seat in the hotel's lobby, collecting stories for his daily column, aptly titled, "Village Gossip." A painting of Dunne sitting at his post still hangs above his chair in the lobby. (Courtesy of the Museum of New Mexico, Photo Archives, No. 10701.)

LA FONDA'S INTERIOR PATIO, C. 1930. Hotel guests and local residents were frequently entertained by New Mexico singers and dancers in La Fonda's interior patio. The Santa Fe Fiesta's fashion show was often held at the hotel, as was the fiesta's Conquistadores Ball. As the social center of Santa Fe, the hotel hosted parties throughout the year. La Fonda's Halloween party in October 1932 had a jungle theme, with appropriate music and decorations provided by La Fonda's staff. According to a newspaper description of the festivities, 500 guests attended in outfits ranging from a parrot costume, worn by artist Will Shuster, to a tiger costume, worn by a woman "with a magnificent tail that wagged as she walked." (Courtesy of the Museum of New Mexico, Photo Archives, Nos. 23098 and 54330.)

LA FONDA GUEST ROOM, C. 1940. La Fonda hosted countless celebrities, including political leaders John F. Kennedy and Eleanor Roosevelt; authors Willa Cather and Sinclair Lewis; and actors Clint Eastwood, Errol Flynn, Dennis Hopper, Diane Keaton, Robert Redford, and James Stewart. In addition to its thousands of guests, La Fonda became the long-term residence of several well-respected men and women. Mary Stauffer Naylor lived in Suite 410 from 1963 to 1982.

ANOTHER LA FONDA GUEST ROOM, C. 1940. La Fonda has been the honeymoon destination for many newlyweds. Some couples returned to celebrate milestone anniversaries. In 1937, Elmer and Pearl Moore honeymooned at La Fonda, spending $5 a night for Room 236. In 1987, the romantic couple celebrated their golden wedding anniversary by returning to La Fonda, staying in the same room, and paying the same price thanks to the hotel's generous manager.

LA FONDA'S DINNER MENU AND DINING ROOM, C. 1940. Most of La Fonda's commercial art of the 1930s was printed by Santa Fe's most famous woodcut artist, Willard Clark. According to Clark's biographer, David Farmer, La Fonda's guests could sit at dinner tables with decorative place mats, order from colorful menus, sleep in beds with painted headboards, and hang "Do Not Disturb" signs on their doors—all with items designed and printed by Clark in his distinctive Southwest style. (Courtesy of L. A. Reed.)

H-3971   Dining Room, La Fonda Hotel   Santa Fe, New Mexico

LA FONDA'S STAFF, 1930S. La Fonda was known for the longevity of its loyal, hard-working staff. Konrad Allgaier served as La Fonda's head chef for over three decades. Feliciana "Chanita" Leyba worked in the hotel's kitchen for 52 years. Amarante "Monte" Chavez started as a pantry worker in 1929 before becoming the hotel restaurant's maître d', a job he held until his retirement in 1989. Front desk manager Russell Wilson served until the late 1960s; his portrait (left) still hangs in the hotel's lobby. Bell captain Adelaido "Lalo" Ortega worked for over 50 years. Ernesto Martinez, the hotel's resident artist, has left his trademark flowers and designs nearly everywhere in La Fonda during a career that now spans five decades. (Courtesy of the Museum of New Mexico, Photo Archives, No. 55735, and La Fonda History Collection.)

Five

ALBUQUERQUE
THE ALVARADO HOTEL

THE ALVARADO, ALBUQUERQUE, NEW MEXICO, C. 1905. Originally a simple eating house opened in 1883, the Harvey House operation in Albuquerque was rebuilt on a grand scale at a cost of $200,000 ($4.2 million in today's money). The new Harvey House opened with considerable fanfare on May 11, 1902. Using Mission Revival architecture, Charles F. Whittlesey designed the hotel, while Mary Colter designed its interior as her first job for the Fred Harvey Company. As the Harvey Company's largest rail-side hotel (with 119 guest rooms), the Alvarado was named for Hernando de Alvarado, who had explored the Southwest with Francisco Coronado on the latter's famous expedition of 1540 to 1542. (Courtesy of the Albuquerque Museum Photo Collection, No. PA1982.180.218.)

ALVARADO'S INDIAN ARTS BUILDING, C. 1915 AND 1925. Tourists examine Native American wares outside the Alvarado's Indian Arts Building. Passengers arrived in Albuquerque to find Native American venders displaying their arts and crafts on traditional blankets. This particular postcard was so popular that it was reissued several times, with the tourists' clothing altered to reflect different styles in different decades. Those who received this postcard saw a culturally interesting but clearly nonthreatening image of the Southwest.

THE ALVARADO'S INDIAN ARTS BUILDING, C. 1915. Proceeding past the Native American venders they met on arrival at the Alvarado, passengers entered the hotel's Indian Arts Building. Designed by Mary Colter and Fred Harvey's daughter Minnie Harvey Huckel, the building included a museum of carefully selected Native American art (not for sale), as well as a salesroom stocked with arts and crafts available for purchase at reasonable prices. The Harvey Company's Indian Department bought large quantities of Native American pottery, baskets, jewelry, and rugs, creating a valuable new market for Native American craftsmen—as well as for the Fred Harvey Company. Headed by Fred Harvey's son-in-law John Frederick Huckel and managed by Herman Schweizer, the Indian Department purchased almost 4,000 Navajo textiles in 1908 and 1909 alone. But the impact of Harvey Company purchases was not always positive. Traditional designs and colors were often compromised in the interest of tourist demands. As Schweizer told a supplier of Native American crafts, "We have got to get up something new all the time to keep the public interested so they will buy."

NATIVE AMERICAN DEMONSTRATORS, C. 1910. The Harvey Company found that Native American craft sales increased considerably when tourists watched artists demonstrate their skills (ideally with Native American children present) in a special workroom in the Indian Arts Building. Elle, a Navajo weaver, was the most popular Indian demonstrator. The Harvey Company appreciated Elle and her husband Tom's willingness to live in Albuquerque when few Navajos agreed to prolonged periods of separation from their reservation.

ELLE AND THE HARVEY COMPANY, C. 1906. Elle was willing to have her picture taken when many Native Americans believed that their spirits would be lost if their images were taken in photographs. At least 50 images of Elle appeared on Santa Fe postcards, in promotional brochures, on a magazine cover, in a movie filmed at the Alvarado, and even on playing cards. Elle worked for the Harvey Company from 1902 to 1923.

NAVAJOS PARADE PAST WEST SIDE OF THE ALVARADO AT THE START OF THE MONTEZUMA BALL, C. 1915. The Alvarado was the scene of many important social events, including the Montezuma Ball that was held to formally dedicate the hotel in 1902 and each year during the territorial (later state) fair until 1917. Historian Mo Palmer stated that each Montezuma Ball began with an elaborate parade, much dancing (including scandalous new dances like the Castle Canter), and a "delicious plate supper" served by Harvey Girls. The hotel was the scene of many other special events, from banquets and proms to weddings and anniversaries. In the opinion of many Albuquerque residents, it was the place to go and the place to be seen in local society. (Courtesy of the Albuquerque Museum Photo Collection, No. PA1982.180.210.)

THE ALVARADO'S LOBBY, C. 1925.
In 1957, Walter McNally, the Alvarado's chief clerk, retired after 45 years. Upon retiring, McNally declared, "I have enjoyed every minute of my career. In the hotel business [you] meet people . . . from all walks of life." Harvey House clerks were so honest that they were known to rush after guests who accidentally left their wallets after checking out at the hotel's front desk. (Courtesy of L. A. Reed.)

ALVARADO BELLBOYS, 1912.
According to the *Albuquerque Morning Journal*, bellboys did so well at the Alvarado and other city hotels that hotel owners in the 1910s were "thinking seriously of trading places with them." The *Journal* reported that in the busiest hotel seasons bellboys averaged $4 to $5 in tips per day (equal to about $100 in today's money). (Courtesy of the Museum of New Mexico, Photo Archives, No. 158487.)

ALVARADO GUEST BILL, JULY 6, 1955.
The Alvarado offered as many as 119
guest rooms. For his single room, guest
Joseph F. Anderson paid $6.50, or $49 in
today's money, each night. Combined with
some meals and a bar tab from his first night
in town, Anderson's seven-day bill equaled
$59.18, or $451.70 today.

**ALVARADO GUEST ROOM
KEY.** As at La Fonda, several
residents lived at the Alvarado,
including painter Carl von
Hassler, respected as the "dean
of the Albuquerque art colony."
While maintaining a home in
Georgetown near Washington,
D. C., Sen. Dennis Chavez
and his wife often stayed
at the Alvarado when they
returned to Albuquerque during
Chavez's long career in the
U.S. Senate, from 1935 to 1962.

ALVARADO'S 120-SEAT DINING ROOM, 1908. Many Albuquerque families ate at the Alvarado so often that they each had their "reserved" tables. Local residents recall that it could take up to half an hour to get to a table because they had to stop and visit with so many friends and relatives upon entering the large dining facility for Sunday lunch. (Courtesy of the Albuquerque Museum Photo Collection, No. PA1972.031.017.)

ALVARADO'S 116-SEAT LUNCHROOM, C. 1935. Harvey Houses were known to help destitute travelers. During the Great Depression, a mother and her children were almost penniless when they ordered small meals at the Alvarado. Recognizing the family's plight, the manager paid their bill and sent them off with bags of extra food. Opening the bags, the woman exclaimed, "Loaves and fishes, loaves and fishes." (Courtesy of the Albuquerque Museum Photo Collection, No. PA1982.180.203.)

THE ALVARADO
ALBUQUERQUE.N.M.
FRED HARVEY

BREAKFAST

Strawberries

Baked Apples   Sliced Oranges   Stewed Rhubarb

Stewed Prunes   Marmalade

Grape Nuts   Toasted Corn Flakes

Corn Meal Mush   Puffed Rice   Shredded Wheat

Oatmeal Porridge

Kippered Herring

Boiled Salt Mackerel   Broiled Lake Trout

Broiled Pork Tenderloin
Fried Chicken, plain

Corned Beef Hash   Calf's Liver and Bacon

French Toast   Fried Mush with Jelly

Eggs as Ordered

Breakfast Bacon   Broiled Mutton Chops   Broiled Ham

Potatoes:

Baked   German Fried   French Fried

Corn Muffins   Dry or Buttered Toast   Hot Rolls

Tea   Coffee   Cocoa

Monday, June 7, 1915.

For Mineral Waters, see Wine Card

ALVARADO BREAKFAST MENU, JUNE 7, 1915. Never willing to compromise on good, fresh food for Harvey House meals, Fred Harvey procured his food from local farmers, distant suppliers (with goods delivered twice weekly in special refrigerated freight cars), and the company's own ranch (in Colorado), farm (in Arizona), and dairies (in Arizona and New Mexico). On the eve of World War I, Harvey Houses used 5 million pounds of potatoes, 1.5 million pounds of sugar, 500,000 pounds of butter, 750,000 chickens, and 500,000 pounds of coffee (enough for about 20 million cups) per year. Chefs sent daily reports from each Harvey House to company headquarters in Kansas City to assure that supplies were adequate and meal portions were consistently generous. Carefully planned daily menus were sent to all Harvey Houses so that travelers never saw the same meal choices more than once on each trip on the Santa Fe. (Courtesy of L. A. Reed.)

ELLE AND A BLANKET FOR PRES. TEDDY ROOSEVELT, MAY 1903. Elle, the Navajo weaver who often demonstrated her skills at the Alvarado, was asked to weave a Navajo blanket for the local Commercial Club to present as a unique gift to President Roosevelt during his 1903 visit to New Mexico; she completed the task in less than a week. Pres. William Howard Taft was similarly honored during his visit to the Alvarado in October 1909. A banquet for Taft and 65 territorial leaders was held in the hotel's grand dining room. According to one unverified report, the overweight Taft got stuck in an Alvarado bathtub during his short stay in Albuquerque. It is not known if President Taft recalled this embarrassing moment on January 6, 1912, the day he signed New Mexico's long-awaited statehood bill. (Courtesy of Nancy Tucker.)

MOVIE STARS, C. 1925. Hollywood stars such as Lois Wilson (right), Douglas Fairbanks Jr., and Mary Pickford (below, with Albuquerque mayor Clyde Tingley) frequented the Alvarado. A short silent movie was shot at the Alvarado in September 1912. According to the *Albuquerque Morning Journal*, "The Alvarado hotel was realistically held up in all the approved style of cowboys, big six-shooters, frightened tourists, and everything else that ought to go [into a] representation of the Easterner's idea of what the wild West really is." First called *Holding Up Tourists at the Alvarado Hotel*, the movie's name was later shortened to *The Tourist*, undoubtedly since the original title would have been detrimental to the hotel's future tourist trade. (Courtesy of the Albuquerque Museum Photo Collection, Nos. PA1982.128.111 and PA1991.002.004.)

ALVARADO FOUNTAIN, GARDEN, AND PORCH, C. 1933. While most visitors enjoyed their stay at the Alvarado, some, like Secretary of the Interior Harold Ickes, did not. After attending a dinner held in his honor in the Alvarado's dining room on June 4, 1939, Ickes wrote in his diary that he retired to his guest room, where he spent "one of the worst [nights] I have had for a long time. It was stifling hot . . . and very noisy. Every train on the Santa Fe stops at Albuquerque, and the Alvarado is right on the tracks." After attending additional ceremonies the following day, Ickes "went back to the hotel where I managed to have a better night with the help of [an] electric fan." (Courtesy of L. A. Reed and the Albuquerque Museum Photo Collection, No. PA1978.141.315.)

Six

ATTERED GEMS
Y HOUSES OF CENTRAL
OUTHERN NEW MEXICO

GRAN QUIVIRA, CLOVIS, NEW MEXICO, C. 1915. Clovis's Harvey House was designed by Santa Fe staff architect Myron Church, employing the same Mission Revival style he used in designing other Harvey Houses at Vaughn and Belen. Clovis's house was named for an abandoned Tompiro Indian pueblo, located hundreds of miles to the west. The hotel, with 35 guest rooms, a 54-seat lunchroom, and a 94-seat dining room, opened on August 15, 1912. Harvey Houses like the Gran Quivira greeted train passengers with a rail-side sign featuring the Santa Fe logo and the Harvey House's particular name. With Harvey's national reputation, these signs were like seals of approval, guaranteeing guests that they would receive only the best in food and service. (Courtesy of L. A. Reed.)

HARVEY HOUSE UNDER CONSTRUCTION VAUGHN, N.M.

LOS CHAVEZ UNDER CONSTRUCTION IN VAUGHN, NEW MEXICO, OCTOBER 24, 1910. Designed by Myron Church in Mission Revival style architecture, Los Chavez was named after the powerful Chavez family, who had arrived in New Mexico during the Spanish conquest led by Don Juan de Oñate in 1598. With only 11 guest rooms, Los Chavez was only slightly larger than Lamy's eight-room El Ortiz. Seldom hosting overnight travelers, Los Chavez served as a dorm for local teachers; seven of its guest rooms were normally reserved for teachers who taught at the nearby public school. (Courtesy of L. A. Reed.)

LOS CHAVEZ'S EXTERIOR, STAFF, AND LUNCHROOM, 1911. Alice Garnas fondly remembered her two years as a Harvey Girl in Vaughn in the late 1920s. Alice told historian Lesley Poling-Kempes that she felt so "respected and protected" at Los Chavez that, while other girls sought transfers to more exciting Harvey House locations, Alice was content to stay in Vaughn. Alice's most famous customer was Charles Lindbergh, whose plane had been forced to land near Vaughn in 1928. While her fellow Harvey Girls "practically fought over who would serve him," the house manager chose Alice to be the pilot's waitress at each meal. Alice described Lindbergh as "friendly and very nice, although . . . very shy and quiet." (Courtesy of L. A. Reed and the University of Arizona, Special Collections, AZ326, Box 8, Folder 7.)

HARVEY HOUSE, BELEN, NEW MEXICO, C. 1915. As in Clovis and Vaughn, Belen's Harvey House was designed in Mission Revival architecture by Santa Fe Railway architect Myron Church. Joseph E. Nelson and Sons of Chicago completed the restaurant's construction by December 1910. Far less expensive than larger Harvey Houses like the Alvarado, Belen's structure cost $25,800, or almost $560,000 in today's money. With no guest rooms (its upstairs rooms were used to house its Harvey Girls and house manager), this Harvey House's sole purpose was to serve good food in its 45-seat lunchroom and 64-seat dining room.

BELEN HARVEY HOUSE FLOOR PLANS, BASED ON ORIGINAL 1910 BLUEPRINTS. Like all Harvey Houses, the one in Belen served as its local community's social center for many important activities, from business banquets to high school proms. It also served the local population's daily needs. A prominent businessman sat at the same lunchroom seat, read his daily newspaper, and ordered the same menu items each weekday morning for years. When teenagers of the 1930s went to Saturday night dances, they often ended their evenings at the Harvey House where "big spenders" bought their dates Cokes for the princely sum of a dime. (Courtesy of Brian Garrett and Alex Sanchez.)

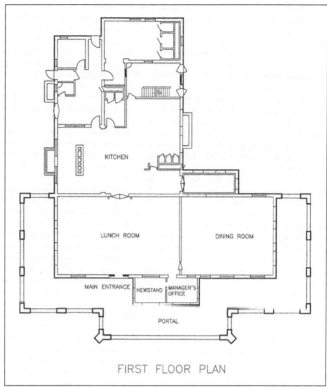

FIRST FLOOR PLAN

SECOND FLOOR PLAN

No. R 167

SANTA FE ROUTE EATING HOUSES.

COMPANY REDUCED RATE PERMIT, ENTITLING

MR. L. K. Ruble,

Traveling Auditor.

To Meals at 50 Cts. Each at all Houses Until Dec. 31, 1901,
Unless Otherwise Ordered,

Fred, Harvey

RAILROAD WORKER'S MEAL TICKET, C. 1901. Belen Harvey Girl Ruth Armstrong remembers that when not serving local residents and railroad passengers from "meal trains," the Harvey House staff kept busy feeding railroad workers, called "rails." Ruth recalls that rails sometimes teased and could be rough, but most were kind and generous. Harvey Houses were often located at railroad division points where Santa Fe workers laid over between shifts. To help defray the cost of these layovers, the railroad provided coupons (called "pie books") that allowed for generous worker discounts on all meals served in Harvey Houses. (Courtesy of L. A. Reed.)

NEWSSTANDS AT BELEN'S HARVEY HOUSE AND AT LA CASTAÑEDA, C. 1925. Dissatisfied with the service and merchandise offered by independent newsstand operators, the Santa Fe turned to the Harvey Company to run yet another essential business for the comfort and convenience of travelers. Typical of every Harvey newsstand, Belen's Harvey House sold everything from newspapers and magazines to Fred Harvey postcards and a variety of cigars. As in Belen, most Harvey newsstands were located within Harvey House lunchrooms for easy customer access. Other newsstands were located outside, closer to the tracks, as at La Castañeda (below). Newsstand personnel were instructed to give the buyer of a single newspaper the same attention they would give the buyer of the most expensive item among their merchandise. (Courtesy of the University of Arizona, Special Collections, AZ326, Box 7, Folder 8, and Box 8, Folder 3.)

Harvey House, San Marcial, N. Mex.

HARVEY HOUSE, SAN MARCIAL, NEW MEXICO, C. 1912. The Harvey House in San Marcial opened in 1883 with only seven guest rooms and 27 lunchroom seats. San Marcial thrived as a small railroad community until the summer of 1929. In that tragic season, two floods inundated the town, leaving wide paths of destruction in their wake. So many people rushed to the town's aid in the flood of mid-August that the Harvey House staff, including five dedicated Harvey Girls, served an estimated 600 customers in a 24-hour period. Six weeks later a second flood hit the area, washing out 51 miles of track and toppling entire train engines. Taking refuge on the second floor of the Harvey House, several dozen marooned survivors played music on a portable phonograph to distract themselves through the night until they were rescued the following day. While all humans survived the successive disasters, San Marcial and its Harvey House were lost, never to be repopulated or rebuilt. (Courtesy of L. A. Reed.)

HARVEY HOUSE, RINCON, NEW MEXICO, C. 1910. Opening in 1883, Rincon's small Harvey House had 11 guest rooms and 30 lunchroom seats. Most lunchroom customers were gentlemen, but some were not. Harvey Girl Margaret King Beahler recalled one customer who complained that she must be "sweet on" some members of a railroad crew because she had spent more time serving them than she had spent serving him. In response, Margaret picked up a pie and threw it at the offensive traveler, hitting him square in the face. Having witnessed the incident, Margaret's house manager ordered the customer to leave the premises because no man could insult a Harvey Girl as he had. Managers found it harder to defend other Harvey Girls. A minor crime spree began at the Rincon Harvey House in 1910 when a Harvey Girl stole $40 and a diamond ring from a fellow Harvey Girl's trunk. The culprit proceeded to Deming where another Harvey Girl soon discovered that she was missing a $50 brooch. The female thief was finally apprehended in Silver City. (Courtesy of L. A. Reed.)

HARVEY HOUSE AND DEPOT, DEMING, NEW MEXICO, C. 1910. Originally housed in two boxcars, Deming's new Harvey House opened in 1883, flanked by the Southern Pacific Railroad's offices on one side and the Santa Fe Railroad's offices on the other. Harvey Girls lived on the second floor above the usually busy lunchroom. (Courtesy of L. A. Reed.)

DEMING'S HARVEY HOUSE LUNCHROOM, C. 1910. The Deming Harvey House was one of the only Harvey restaurants ever to be robbed. On Saturday, August 20, 1904, a masked man dressed as a woman and armed with a revolver robbed the Deming establishment of $22.50. Discarding his poor disguise, Edward Scarborough foolishly returned to the scene of the crime, was recognized, and was placed under arrest. Ten years later, Pancho Villa, the Harvey House's most notorious visitor, ate breakfast at the Deming restaurant, but did not rob it. Accompanied by 35 bodyguards, Villa addressed a large crowd at the depot, promising that the Mexican Revolution would soon end and peace would return to the U.S.-Mexico border. Not true to his word, Villa and his men returned to the border and all but destroyed the neighboring town of Columbus, New Mexico, on March 9, 1916. (Courtesy of L. A. Reed.)

HARVEY GIRL MILDRED CLARK, 1920. Although most Harvey Girls led highly moral lives during and after their Harvey House careers, there were exceptions. Having lied to gain employment to help care for an ailing sister, Mildred Clark began her career as a 14-year-old Harvey Girl at the Deming Harvey House. Mildred learned several valuable lessons during her brief time in Harvey's service. In particular, she learned the best ways to impress customers and ensure good tips, especially from admiring males. Exploiting her special appeal to men, Mildred soon left her job as a Harvey Girl and entered what is known as the world's oldest profession. After many years and adventures, Mildred Clark is best remembered as Madame Millie, the most famous woman of ill repute in New Mexico history. (Courtesy of the Max Evans Collection.)

ORIGINAL HARVEY HOUSE, GALLUP, NEW MEXICO, C. 1910. Harvey Company supervisors were known to suddenly appear for surprise inspections in any Harvey House, including the one in Gallup. Employees kept on their best behavior, lest they be fired for one of many possible infractions. Leery of such inspections and their consequences, house managers developed a telegraphic code to warn fellow managers when inspectors were known to be en route. (Courtesy of L. A. Reed.)

GALLUP HARVEY HOUSE AND DEPOT FIRE, JANUARY 6, 1914. A disastrous fire began in Gallup's Harvey House basement about 10:30 p.m. The blaze spread quickly, reaching the roof within 15 minutes. Despite the "valiant work" of Gallup's fire department, the Harvey House, freight house, and parts of the depot were destroyed at a property loss of over $100,000 (more than $2 million in today's money). (Courtesy of L. A. Reed.)

H-1882 EL NAVAJO, FRED HARVEY HOTEL, GALLUP, NEW MEXICO   (AFTER PAINTING BY FRED GEARY)

EL NAVAJO, GALLUP'S NEW HARVEY HOUSE, POSTCARD FROM A PAINTING BY FRED GEARY, 1923. The Harvey House used temporary quarters after the fire of 1914. Plans for Gallup's new railroad facilities had been drawn up by early 1917, but delays caused by World War I and other factors prevented the new establishment's completion until 1923. Costing $250,000 (or $3 million in today's money), the new Harvey House was designed by Mary Colter using a rather modern version of Pueblo Revival architecture. Named to celebrate the nearby Navajo Reservation and to lure cultural tourists, El Navajo opened just eight months after Gallup's first Inter-Tribal Indian Ceremonial was held in 1922. Ready to help accommodate the hundreds of guests who attended the ceremonials each year, El Navajo offered 71 guest rooms, while its lunchroom sat 81 travelers, and its dining room sat an additional 112.

EL NAVAJO'S OPENING CEREMONIES. Unlike most Southwestern Harvey Houses, with their emphasis on Hispanic culture and design, El Navajo focused on only Native American motifs. In fact, Mary Colter, who designed the hotel's unique interior, received special permission to use sacred Navajo sand paintings as decorative motifs throughout the building. Navajo medicine men selected and helped create El Navajo's sand paintings, normally used only for religious ceremonies and then destroyed. In keeping with Navajo tradition, a house blessing was conducted by several Navajo medicine men who offered special prayers and sprinkled sacred pollen over the new dwelling and its owners (or at least Harvey Company officials) at El Navajo's opening ceremonies on May 25, 1923. An estimated 2,000 people attended the event. (Courtesy of L. A. Reed and the Museum of New Mexico, Photo Archives, No. 151551.)

THE SAND-PAINTINGS
OF THE NAVAJO

*The meaning and purpose of the sacred art
of the Medicine Men as exemplified
by authentic reproductions
on the walls of*

EL NAVAJO
SANTA FE HOTEL
GALLUP, NEW MEXICO

*With a brief description of "The Blessing-
of-the-House" Ceremony of May 25, 1923*

Published by
FRED HARVEY
KANSAS CITY, MISSOURI

EL NAVAJO'S LOBBY, C. 1923. When Ellen Hunt was hired as a Harvey Girl, she was asked if she was afraid of Native Americans. Saying no (she had known only two in her life back East), Ellen was sent to El Navajo and, like most Harvey Girls, got along well with Gallup's diverse population. Harvey Girls gladly exchanged their uniforms for Southwestern velvet outfits and Native American jewelry during the annual Inter-Tribal Ceremonials.

EL NAVAJO'S DINING ROOM, 1927. To encourage gentlemanly behavior, males were required to wear suit jackets in Harvey House dining rooms. If tourists lacked such attire, each house kept a small stock of alpaca coats. Harvey's "coat rule" was legally challenged in Oklahoma in 1921. Oklahoma's Supreme Court decided in the company's favor, finding the rule to be in the best interest of "civilized society." (Courtesy of L. A. Reed.)

Seven

LIKE INDIAN BEADS
HARVEY HOUSES OF ARIZONA
AND SOUTHERN CALIFORNIA

ORIGINAL HARVEY HOUSE, WINSLOW, ARIZONA, C. 1910. Located 133 miles west of Gallup and opened in 1887, most of Winslow's first Harvey House burned in yet another Harvey House fire in 1914. Fires were tragic but regular occurrences in the late 19th and early 20th centuries, especially in wood-frame restaurants where kitchen accidents and other mishaps often took place. (Courtesy of L. A. Reed)

WINSLOW'S NEW HARVEY HOUSE, LA POSADA, C. 1930. Opened on May 15, 1930, Winslow's new 62-room hotel and 116-seat restaurant was the last Harvey House built in the Southwest. Designed by Mary Colter, La Posada was said to have been her favorite Harvey project. Meaning "The Inn" or "resting place" in Spanish, La Posada was built to resemble a hospitable old Spanish hacienda. The Harvey Company had originally planned to call its new enterprise El Ranchito, until a telegram from Winslow businessmen warned company officials that El Ranchito was a term frequently used for houses of ill repute along the Mexican border. The company quickly found an alternate name with a far more wholesome identity. (Courtesy of the Museum of New Mexico, Photo Archives, No. 53652.)

H-4157   PASSAGEWAY TO WEST WING, LA POSADA, FRED HARVEY HOTEL, WINSLOW, ARIZONA

LA POSADA INTERIORS, C. 1930. In keeping with her focus on Southwestern culture, Mary Colter filled La Posada with Spanish arches, long corridors, and an array of antique Spanish furniture, including a 200-year-old wooden chest. Even new furniture was made to look antique by craftsmen working in an on-site wood shop. With her usual attention to detail, Colter covered guest room floors with Navajo rugs trampled on by construction workers to make the floor coverings look old and used. (Courtesy of L. A. Reed.)

H-4159   THE LOUNGE, LA POSADA, FRED HARVEY HOTEL, WINSLOW, ARIZONA

H-4158 DINING ROOM, LA POSADA, FRED HARVEY HOTEL, WINSLOW, ARIZONA

LA POSADA'S DINING ROOM, C. 1930. In designing La Posada's dining room, Mary Colter included a tile mural (left) honoring San Pasqual, the patron saint of feasts. Because the Harvey Girls' traditional black and white uniforms were too severe for La Posada's traditional Hispanic setting, Harvey Girls in Winslow eventually wore uniforms with colorful aprons featuring cacti, donkeys, and other Southwestern icons.

LA POSADA'S GARDEN PATIO, C. 1950. La Posada's most famous guests included presidents Franklin D. Roosevelt and Harry Truman; aviators Amelia Earhart and Charles Lindbergh; and movie stars like Will Rogers and John Wayne. Harvey Girl Zada Sharon remembered serving Clark Gable. When the famous guest left a silver dollar as a tip, many people "wanted to buy it, just because Clark Gable had touched it." (Courtesy of L. A. Reed.)

14928 FRAY MARCOS HOTEL, WILLIAMS, ARIZ.   COPR. FRED HARVEY.

FRAY MARCOS, WILLIAMS, ARIZONA, C. 1910. Located 95 miles west of Winslow, Fred Harvey's first eatery in Williams opened in 1894, when the company took over a restaurant that had been in operation since as early as 1884. Renowned architect Francis W. Wilson designed the Harvey Company's new hotel and restaurant, which opened on March 10, 1908. The company named its Harvey House to honor the Spanish Franciscan missionary Fray Marcos de Niza, the first European explorer of Arizona and New Mexico. Returning to New Spain (today's Mexico) in 1539, Fray Marcos reported that the far northern frontier was rife with wealth and opportunity for Spanish conquest.

THE FRAY MARCOS'S LOBBY AND INDIAN ROOM, C. 1910. Fray Marcos offered 22 guest rooms (and 10 Harvey Girl dorm rooms) when it opened in 1908. Responding to increased business in the prosperous 1920s, the Harvey Company built a two-story addition, with 21 new guest rooms, in 1925. Guests often stayed at the Fray Marcos en route to the Grand Canyon either by train (a 63-mile spur line to the South Rim had opened on September 17, 1901) or by car (a good road had been completed soon after the Grand Canyon was designated as a national park in 1919).

A Japanese Bellboy at Fray Marcos, c. 1925. This rare postcard was signed, "Sincerely Yours, Frank Stalas." Stalas probably gave guests autographed copies of his souvenir postcard to remind them of his good service and to encourage generous gratuities. The Harvey Company often hired foreign-born bellboys in places like Williams and the Grand Canyon to better serve its many international guests. (Courtesy of L. A. Reed.)

THE ESCALANTE, ASH FORK, ARIZONA, C. 1910. The original Harvey House in Ash Fork, a wooden structure that had opened in 1895, burned to the ground in a fire that started in the restaurant's kitchen on June 17, 1905. A new, more impressive Harvey House was built at a cost of $115,000 ($2.6 million in today's money) and named after yet another Spanish explorer, Francisco Silvestre Velez Escalante, a Franciscan missionary who traveled through the Southwest in 1776. The Escalante boasted 23 guest rooms as well as seating for 62 at its lunchroom and 120 more customers in its dining room. (Courtesy of Marshall Trimble.)

THE ESCALANTE'S LOBBY, C. 1910. Like many large Harvey Houses, the elegant Escalante included not only a lunchroom, a dining room, and a hotel, but also a newsstand, a curio shop (featuring Native American arts and crafts), and a barber shop. The grounds were well landscaped with fountains, flowers, and an extensive cactus garden on the hotel's east side. Despite its interior and exterior beauty, the Escalante was the scene of domestic turmoil soon after it opened in 1905. According to historian Marshall Trimble, a distraught woman brandished a revolver and chased her husband through the hotel for over an hour before a local deputy disarmed her "in as gentlemanly way as possible." (Courtesy of L. A. Reed.)

THE HAVASU, SELIGMAN, ARIZONA, C. 1910. Seligman's original Harvey eatery had opened in 1895. Reopened as the Havasu in 1905, the new Harvey House was named for the Havasupai Indian tribe. The hotel offered 19 guest rooms, while its lunchroom sat 47 travelers and its dining room sat an additional 80 customers. The Havasu's prairie style architecture was unique among Harvey Houses of the Southwest. (Courtesy of L. A. Reed.)

POSTCARD IN JAPANESE. Reflecting the international clientele of many Harvey Houses, this postcard was bought in Seligman and mailed from Ash Fork in early 1909. The message is typical of tourist postcards, politely inquiring as to the recipient's health and commenting on the weather: "Two or three days ago, it snowed and the ground was completely covered. It feels isolated, but I'm fine." (Courtesy of L. A. Reed; translation by Mark Hedy.)

HARVEY HOUSE EXTERIOR AND LUNCHROOM, KINGMAN, ARIZONA, C. 1910. The Harvey House in Kingman was opened as a 42-seat lunchroom in 1901. In a modern improvement, electric lamps replaced the restaurant's original oil lamps in 1912. A new 63-seat dining room was added during World War I. According to 1929 railroad schedules, a popular Santa Fe passenger train known as *The Missionary* traveled east overnight from California, stopped for breakfast at Kingman, lunch at Ash Fork, and dinner at Winslow before continuing its journey into New Mexico and destinations further east. (Courtesy of the Mohave Museum.)

EL GARCES, NEEDLES, CALIFORNIA, C. 1910. Opened in a wooden structure in 1887, the Harvey eatery in Needles followed the pattern of so many early Harvey establishments by falling victim to fire in 1906. And, as with so many Harvey Houses, a far more elaborate structure rose from the ashes in 1908 at a cost of $250,000 (or more than $5.4 million in today's money).

EL GARCES, NATIVE VENDERS, C. 1910. Needles's new Harvey House was named El Garces after Padre Francisco Garces, a Spanish priest who passed through this region several times while traveling between missions in California and southern Arizona in the 1770s. El Garces opened with 29 guest rooms and seats for as many as 73 customers in its lunchroom and 140 in its dining room.

CASA DEL DESIERTO, BARSTOW, CALIFORNIA, C. 1915. Barstow's first Harvey House opened in May 1887, but burned down just two months later on July 8; it was soon replaced with a new structure. Incredibly, Harvey's eateries in Barstow burned two more times (in 1892 and in 1908), but the Harvey Company continued to build new houses, including its last, which promised to be "thoroughly fireproof" when it opened on February 22, 1911. Designed by Francis W. Wilson in a "Neo Southwestern" style, the Casa del Desierto, or "Desert House," employed 38 able workers in its first summer in operation. Twenty years later, the staff included everyone from house manager Eddie Behean to Orville Lewis, a kitchen helper whose duties included making at least 30 gallons of ice cream per day. Understandably, ice cream was a favorite dessert for guests in Barstow's high desert temperatures. (Courtesy of L. A. Reed.)

H-1236 THE LOBBY, CASA DEL DESIERTO, BARSTOW, CALIF.

CASA DEL DESIERTO, C. 1915. The Casa del Desierto had 30 guest rooms. In 1919, some workers at the Barstow Harvey House took the controversial step of joining a new labor union known as the Hotel and Restaurant Alliance. Strongly opposed to unions, the Harvey Company fired all those who had dared to join the local chapter. There is no record of Harvey Girls or any other Harvey employees striking against their employer. Rather than organize and strike, off-duty Harvey Girls in Barstow were more likely to join desert expeditions, play croquet on hotel grounds, attend local dances, or rent bicycles for short rides through town. With all its outdoor activities, Barstow was a preferred Harvey House assignment despite its desert heat. (Courtesy of L. A. Reed and the University of Arizona, Special Collections, AZ326, Box 3, File 3.)

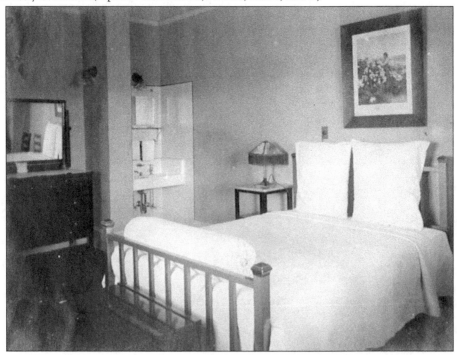

H-1203 LUNCH ROOM, CASA DEL DESIERTO, BARSTOW, CALIF.

CASA DEL DESIERTO, c. 1915. The Casa del Desierto's lunchroom sat 52 customers and its dining room 110. Harvey Houses were known for their many good beverages, but especially for their famous coffee. For the best coffee, Fred Harvey used only the Chase and Sanborn brand. According to railroad historian Lenore Dils, "Whether you had a cup [of Harvey coffee in Kansas City or in] Albuquerque, it tasted exactly the same as the last cup you had many miles away. The reason for this was that Mr. Harvey had the water analyzed at each of his Harvey Houses, and after much experimentation, he worked out an exact formula for each [location]. Whether the water was soft or hard, one still got a superb cup of coffee." (Courtesy of the University of Arizona, Special Collections, AZ326, Box 3, File 3.)

H-3107 SANTA FE STATION, SAN BERNARDINO, CALIFORNIA

SAN BERNARDINO, CALIFORNIA, C. 1920.
San Bernardino's original train depot was a wooden structure that opened in 1886, but it burned on November 16, 1916. The Santa Fe Railway spent $800,000 (or over $12.8 million in today's money) to build a grand new depot, designed by W. A. Mohr, using California Mission style architecture with strong Moorish influences. It opened on July 15, 1918. A Harvey House was added three years later. The *San Bernardino Daily Sun* reported that the new restaurant was so popular that it served over a thousand customers on the Fourth of July in 1921. Six-foot-six-inch John C. Ritchie (pictured) served as the restaurant's chef in the mid-1930s. (Courtesy of the Belen Harvey House Museum.)

Eight

The Grand Canyon
El Tovar Hotel and
Bright Angel Lodge

El Tovar Hotel, Grand Canyon, Arizona. This postcard is based on Louis Akin's 1906 painting, *El Tovar Hotel, Grand Canyon, Arizona.* It is said that Fred Harvey discovered the Grand Canyon. This is, of course, an exaggeration. Native American, Spanish, and U.S. explorers had traversed and admired the canyon for years. In fact, Don Pedro de Tobar, for whom the Harvey resort at the Grand Canyon was named, explored the region as part of Francisco Coronado's expedition of 1540 to 1542. Tobar's report of a great river (the Colorado) to the west led to the first European discovery and exploration of the canyon. The Harvey Company can be credited with promoting the canyon as a major tourist destination so that travelers from around the world could "discover" this natural wonder, while enjoying first-class accommodations within yards of the South Rim, as shown here in Louis Akin's famous painting and postcard. The Santa Fe commissioned other artists, including Thomas Moran and Gerald Cassidy, to paint scenes of the canyon for other promotional purposes, from brochures and lithographs to illustrated books and, starting in 1907, the railroad's famous, widely distributed calendars.

DEPOT AT THE GRAND CANYON, C. 1920. In the 1890s, adventuresome visitors could travel from Flagstaff to the Grand Canyon in 11 hours by stagecoach. The ride cost $20. A 63-mile spur line from Williams, Arizona, was completed in 1901, with the first passenger train arriving at the canyon on September 17, 1901. The three-hour trip from Williams cost just $3.95. In 1909, the Santa Fe Railway built a rustic-looking depot (designed by Francis W. Wilson), seen in the background to the left, which provided easy access to El Tovar. (Courtesy of the Grand Canyon National Park Museum Collection, No. 08441.)

GUESTS ARRIVING AT EL TOVAR, C. 1922. The Harvey Company's grand resort was designed by Charles F. Whittlesey, the same architect who had earlier designed the far-different Alvarado in Albuquerque. El Tovar melded the elegance of a European villa with the rustic nature of an American hunting lodge, allowing European and American tourists to experience new surroundings mixed with a comfortable dose of the familiar during their stay at the Grand Canyon. El Tovar is acknowledged as the forerunner of an architectural style known as National Park Rustic. The hotel's construction cost equaled $250,000, or close to $5.7 million in today's money. Begun in 1903, El Tovar opened on January 14, 1905, amid great expectations by the Harvey Company and its regular guests. (Courtesy of the Grand Canyon National Park Museum Collection, No. 09648.)

EL TOVAR, C. 1905. El Tovar opened in 1905 with 87 guest rooms. Guests paid with the American Plan, which included all meals, rather than the European Plan, which included no meals added to the cost of a room. In 1905, a guest room cost $3.50 to $4.50 per day, or from $79 to $102 in today's money. Although luxurious for its day, El Tovar had only one bath on each of its four floors; guests had to make reservations to enjoy a bath after long days touring the Grand Canyon. (Courtesy of the Grand Canyon National Park Museum Collection, Nos. 09453 and 09457.)

TEDDY ROOSEVELT AND JOHN HANCE, C. 1911. In 1903, while still president, Roosevelt praised the Grand Canyon's beauty as "absolutely unparalleled" in the world. He had only one wish for the people of Arizona: "I hope you will not have a building of any kind, not a summer cottage, a hotel or anything else, to mar the wonderful grandeur . . . of the canyon. Leave it as it is. You cannot improve on it." Devoted to the canyon and its preservation, Roosevelt declared it a National Monument. Despite his original hope, Roosevelt enjoyed El Tovar once it had opened in 1905. His reputation for "roughing it" helped kindle public interest in various parts of the West, especially the Grand Canyon, and, as a result, El Tovar. By 1914, twenty-five thousand tourists visited the canyon each year. (Courtesy of the Grand Canyon National Park Museum Collection, No. 1573.)

GUESTS PREPARE TO TOUR THE SOUTH RIM, C. 1910 AND 1925. The Harvey Company provided automobile tours of the South Rim, leaving El Tovar at 9:30 a.m. and returning at 5:15 p.m. Horses were also available to tour the rim at $5 per day. According to one brochure, "Only those who are vigorous and in the best physical condition" should attempt to walk on their own in the canyon's 7,000-foot altitude. Many tourists took photographs with increasingly popular hand-held Kodak cameras. Their film was developed at El Tovar's busy newsstand. (Courtesy of the Museum of New Mexico, Photo Archives, 046875.)

H-1540 THE LOOKOUT, GRAND CANYON NATIONAL PARK, ARIZONA.

THE LOOKOUT STUDIO AND DESERT VIEW WATCHTOWER, C. 1935. Guests who toured the Grand Canyon often stopped at several impressive structures designed by Mary Colter, including Hermit's Rest and the Lookout Studio, opened in 1914; Phantom Ranch, opened in 1922; and the Watchtower, dedicated with a Hopi blessing in 1933. Colter designed each building to blend into its surroundings, as if it was a natural extension of the canyon. The Watchtower's interior was decorated with murals depicting Native American legends, as painted by the famous Hopi artist Fred Kabotie, despite occasional clashes with the fastidious Colter. Critics accused the Harvey Company of building the Lookout Studio to obstruct the nearby Kolb Studio in one of several maneuvers designed to squeeze competing enterprises off the rim and create a monopoly of the canyon tourist trade for itself. The company vehemently denied these charges.

THE WATCHTOWER
GRAND CANYON NATIONAL PARK G29

7514. Hopi House, Grand Canyon, Arizona

HOPI HOUSE AND NATIVE AMERICAN DANCERS, C. 1915. Designed by Mary Colter and largely constructed by Hopi Indians to resemble a typical dwelling at Arizona's ancient Oraibi Pueblo, Hopi House opened as the Grand Canyon's first curio shop on January 1, 1905. This unique building featured Hopi craftsmen, like the famous potter Nampeyo, who demonstrated their skills much as other Native Americans did with similar success at the Alvarado. Hopi artists and their families often lived at Hopi House, adding to the display's authenticity and intrigue for guests staying just yards away at El Tovar. Hopi dancers performed each evening. Although alien to their culture, some Hopi men were persuaded to wear feathered bonnets in order to "look more Indian" and thus please Harvey customers.

H-3630   DANCE OF THE HOPI INDIANS, GRAND CANYON NATIONAL PARK, ARIZONA

ALBERT EINSTEIN AND HIS WIFE, ELSA, 1931. Einstein became one of the most famous visitors to the Grand Canyon where he played the tourist, wearing a Native American headdress and holding a pipe (neither of which related to Hopi culture), while stopping en route by train from California to New York on one of his first trips to the United States. Referring to what he was asked to wear on such occasions, Einstein remarked, "[O]ne has to take it all with good humor." (Courtesy of the Grand Canyon National Park Museum Collection, No. 05118.)

H-4477   DINING ROOM, EL TOVAR HOTEL, GRAND CANYON NATIONAL PARK, ARIZONA

EL TOVAR'S 150-SEAT DINING ROOM, C. 1905. El Tovar was so isolated that it could not be supplied with fresh food as easily as Harvey Houses located along the Santa Fe's main line. As a result, much of El Tovar's fruits and vegetables were grown in nearby greenhouses. A chicken house provided fresh eggs and chickens. A dairy herd gave fresh milk. Other foods were delivered via the railroad's spur line.

EL TOVAR'S KITCHEN, c. 1905. Using pots and pans shown here, chef James Marques prepared such fine dishes as his "Breast of Chicken El Tovar." The recipe called for six whole breasts of chicken, six large mushrooms, one ounce of sherry wine, wild rice, and Hollandaise Sauce as described in George Foster and Peter Weiglin's *Harvey House Cookbook*. (Courtesy of the Grand Canyon National Park Museum Collection, No. 09448.)

HOUSE MANAGER VICTOR PATROSSO WITH HARVEY GIRLS OUTSIDE EL TOVAR, C. 1926. With thousands of international visitors each year, El Tovar's staff was largely international as well. According to the 1910 U.S. Census, 12 of the 17 Harvey Girls employed at El Tovar were the daughters of one or more immigrant parents and 6 of the 17 were born overseas. Sixty-six percent of the rest of El Tovar's staff, from bellboys to chambermaids, had similar foreign origins, making it far easier for them to converse with guests who spoke dozens of languages, including French, German, Russian, and Japanese. House manager Victor Patrosso was typical. A native of Italy, Patrosso worked for the Harvey Company for 40 years (1906–1946), the last 23 of which were spent as El Tovar's manager. Before retiring in 1946, Patrosso used his foreign language skills to host guests from around the world, including international celebrities and members of several royal families. (Courtesy of the Grand Canyon National Park Museum Collection, No. 18350.)

EL TOVAR'S RENDEZVOUS ROOM AND EAST PORCH, C. 1906. After long days touring the Grand Canyon, tourists often gathered to compare their adventures or to write home (via postcards and letters) in El Tovar's Rendezvous Room. Measuring 41 by 37 feet, this large lounge was decorated like a rustic Western hunting lodge, complete with rough pine beams, a huge fireplace, and deer, elk, moose, and buffalo heads mounted on its walls. Other guests preferred to spend their evenings resting on the hotel's wide porch overlooking the nearby canyon. (Courtesy of L. A. Reed and the Grand Canyon National Park Museum Collection, No. 05430.)

BRIGHT ANGEL LODGE UNDER CONSTRUCTION, 1935. The Union Pacific Railroad opened its Grand Canyon Lodge on September 14, 1928. Like so many hotels, it burned in a tragic fire on September 1, 1932. The Santa Fe Railway acquired the property and built a beautiful new facility, designed by architects Francis W. Wilson and Mary Colter. In addition to its main lodge, Bright Angel included both standard and deluxe cabins. With less expensive facilities than those found at El Tovar, Bright Angel offered a viable alternative for budget-minded tourists during (and after) the Great Depression. Named after the nearby Bright Angel Trail, the lodge opened on June 22, 1935. Two thousand guests celebrated the event with a barbecue, cowboy entertainment, and Hopi ceremonial dances. As part of the celebration, Mary Colter decorated the lobby with Western hats, including a sombrero reportedly worn by the Mexican revolutionary leader Pancho Villa. (Courtesy of the Grand Canyon National Park Museum Collection, No. 09707.)

H-4471   ENTRANCE TO BRIGHT ANGEL LODGE, GRAND CANYON NATIONAL PARK, ARIZONA

DRIVEWAY AND MAIN ENTRANCE TO BRIGHT ANGEL LODGE, C. 1936. With its drive-up entrance, separate cabins, and lower prices, Bright Angel was the Harvey facility that most closely resembled modern "auto courts" or motels.

H-4472   THE LOBBY, BRIGHT ANGEL LODGE, GRAND CANYON NATIONAL PARK, ARIZONA

BRIGHT ANGEL LODGE LOBBY, C. 1936. Designed by Mary Colter, the stones used in the 10-foot-high Geological Fireplace were layered in the same sequence in which they were unearthed in the canyon below. Believing that they greatly enhanced a hotel's hospitality, Colter included fireplaces in every Harvey House she designed.

ONE SECTION OF MURAL IN THE BRIGHT ANGEL LODGE BAR, C. 1958. Hopi artist Fred Kabotie painted his humorous image of tourists admiring the canyon from the Bright Angel's patio. While most tourists photograph the canyon, a 20-year-old visitor was so intent on photographing Bright Angel from the South Rim that he backed over the rim and fell to his death in April 1981. (Courtesy of the Grand Canyon National Park Museum Collection, No. 09782c.)

THE DUKE AND DUCHESS OF WINDSOR AT THE GRAND CANYON, 1959. The duke and duchess were only two of the thousands of celebrities who stayed at El Tovar or Bright Angel Lodge, from authors like Zane Grey to no fewer than eight U.S. presidents. (Courtesy of the Grand Canyon National Park Museum Collection, No. 03444.)

INTERIOR OF A BRIGHT ANGEL LODGE CABIN DECORATED BY MARY COLTER, C. 1936. Depending on a guest's budget, Bright Angel offered accommodations for 91 standard or 23 deluxe cabins. No two cabins were alike. One remodeled cabin had been the Red Horse Station, the main terminal for stagecoach travelers visiting the canyon from 1892 to 1902. (Courtesy of the Grand Canyon National Park Museum Collection, No. 8158.)

BUCKEY O'NEILL CABIN, BRIGHT ANGEL LODGE, 1935. Buckey O'Neill built this cabin in the 1890s, making it the oldest structure on the South Rim. Most famous as a Rough Rider in the Spanish-American War, the forward-thinking O'Neill had been among the first to propose the construction of a railroad line to the Grand Canyon. (Courtesy of the Grand Canyon National Park Museum Collection, No. 00628.)

Nine

CULTURAL TOURISM
THE SOUTHWESTERN
INDIAN DETOURS

SOUTHWESTERN INDIAN DETOURS MAGAZINE AD, c. 1928. The Harvey Company hoped to increase bookings at its Harvey Houses by encouraging tourists to alter their travel plans and visit Southwest attractions, from existing pueblos to ancient Native American ruins. Conceived of and managed by Maj. R. Hunter Clarkson, the Southwestern Indian Detours helped boost hotel reservations at La Fonda in Santa Fe by 40 percent from 1927 to 1928; La Fonda underwent major expansion from 1928 to 1929 in response to this new demand. The Alvarado, La Castañeda, and La Posada profited nearly as well. Tourists learned about the Detours in ads run in newspapers, like the *New York Times*, and in magazines, like *Collier's* and *National Geographic*. By early 1928, the Harvey Company was receiving between 8,000 and 10,000 inquiries about the Detours each month, including many from overseas. The Indian Detours seemed a perfect marriage of railroad transportation and its main new competitor, the automobile.

The
Indian,
detour

ANOTHER delightful break in transcontinental rail journey to or from California — either two or three matchless days by motor in the Spanish and Indian country of northern New Mexico.

Santa Fe-Harvey Company management throughout. Rates cover every expense en route for motor transportation, courier service, meals and hotel accommodations with private bath.

2-day Puyé detour $40
3-day Taos-Puyé detour $57.50

mail coupon

Harveycars   Mr. W. J. Black, Pass. Traf. Mgr.,
                          Santa Fe System Lines
1200-A Railway Exchange, Chicago
Am interested in "Indian-detour" and Harveycar
Motor Cruises Off the Beaten Path. Please send detailed
information and descriptive folders.

DETOUR COURIER, C. 1929. Travelers could purchase Southwestern Indian Detour tickets at Santa Fe Railway ticket offices or from young women assigned to Santa Fe trains to befriend tourists and share information about Detour adventures. Known as "couriers," these attractive, congenial, well-educated women wore Southwestern attire, with colorful velvet or corduroy Navajo-style blouses, long skirts, Native American jewelry, and wide-brimmed hats featuring the Detours' famous thunderbird emblem. Couriers also served as hosts and guides on Detour trips, earning $150 a month, with an additional $10 if they spoke a foreign language. Most couriers truly enjoyed their work. As former courier Emily Hahn later wrote, "I enjoyed everything. . . . I would come into the house from a day's guiding thick with dust and my voice reduced to a croak. Off with the uniform, into the rusty bathtub, into clean clothes, and out again . . . to a party [in Santa Fe] or a moonlight horseback ride and picnic. I simply never got tired." (Courtesy of Nancy Tucker.)

EDGAR L. HEWETT TRAINING COURIERS, CHACO CANYON, C. 1929. Couriers learned about Southwestern cultures and history in classes conducted in the field (as pictured) and at La Fonda. These special classes, organized by New Mexico author Erna Fergusson, were taught by such renowned archeologists as Edgar L. Hewett and Alfred V. Kidder. Couriers also received *Courier Education Bulletins*, featuring answers to often-asked tourist questions, such as: Are there schools in the pueblos? Are there stores in the pueblos? Do the pueblo families own their own houses? Do all the pueblo Indians speak the same language? Where do they send Indians who have committed murder? And, do they have a right to vote for president? (Courtesy of the Museum of New Mexico, Photo Archives, No. 81763.)

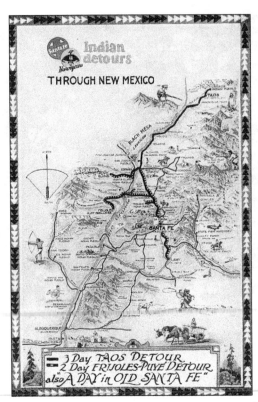

DETOUR ROUTES AND DEPARTURE, c. 1928. A typical three-day detour included: Day one, leave La Castañeda at 9:00 a.m., tour en route to Santa Fe, arrive at La Fonda, 3:30 p.m., dinner at 6:00 p.m.; day two, leave La Fonda at 9:00 a.m., tour northern pueblos and ruins; arrive back at La Fonda at 4:00 p.m., dinner at 6:00 p.m.; day three, leave La Fonda at 9:00 a.m., tour southern pueblos, arrive at the Alvarado at 5:30 p.m., dinner at 6:30 p.m., tour the Indian Arts Building; depart by train the following morning. The Detours' maiden trip left La Castañeda on May 15, 1926. Detour drivers resembled Western movie stars, complete with cowboy shirts, silk neckerchiefs, and 10-gallon hats. (Courtesy of L. A. Reed and the Museum of New Mexico, Photo Archives, No. 46964.)

PUEBLO INDIAN GREETING DUDES AND DRIVER, C. 1928. In the words of a tourist who described his visit to Santa Clara Pueblo in July 1931, "We got a great kick out of their pottery, homes made of adobe, children, etc. . . . It has been a marvelous day . . . weather just right." While kindling a new interest in native arts, preserving ancient Native American skills, and providing a new source of income, tourist trade came with a cost for the pueblos. As historians Richard and Shirley Cushing Flint point out, "Overly inquisitive and sometimes insensitive travelers [often] invaded the long held privacy of cultural traditions and village life." (Courtesy of the Museum of New Mexico, Photo Archives, No. 132442.)

TOURIST AND NATIVE AMERICAN POTTER, C. 1928. Most tourists retained positive memories of their Indian Detours. As with every Harvey House and service, travelers felt like they were experiencing new, interesting adventures while enjoying safe, comfortable, clean facilities. In 1936, Margaret Fischer was so impressed by her Indian Detour that she did exactly what the Santa Fe Railway and the Harvey Company hoped she would do on her return home to Chicago. As she wrote in a letter to Santa Fe officials, "My . . . evenings at home have been completely taken up entertaining relatives, friends, and acquaintances who have come visiting with the expressed purpose of obtaining all the details of my . . . wonderful vacation." Hearing of her adventures in the Southwest, Margaret's nightly guests may well have signed up for their own Detours in the months and years to come.

Ten

END OF AN ERA
1945–1970

BELEN HARVEY HOUSE, CLOSED IN 1938. Harvey Houses in the Southwest reached their peak of popularity and success in the Harvey Company's golden age, from 1900 to 1929. Unfortunately, the company began to decline by the early 1930s for three main reasons. First, the Great Depression of the 1930s took a heavy toll on both business and vacation travel in the Southwest. Nine Harvey Houses, at Belen, Colorado Springs, Deming, Kingman, Lamy, Rincon, San Marcial, Trinidad, and Vaughn, closed down between 1929 and 1939. Hearing that their house was about to close, Harvey Girls in Belen offered to work for just their room, board, and tips. The Harvey Company refused, making tough, but necessary business decisions in Belen and elsewhere.

EL ORIENTE COURT, 4101 East Central (U. S. Highway 66)
Albuquerque, New Mexico

ROUTE 66 MOTEL, ALBUQUERQUE, C. 1940. The second reason why many Harvey Houses suffered serious decline by the 1930s was because travelers often chose newer, often more convenient means of transportation, especially cars and buses, on new highways, Route 66 in particular. New diners and motels served thousands of automobile travelers. Harvey Houses literally faced the wrong direction, toward the tracks rather than towards the roads that best served modern motorists.

KACHINA ROOM, ALBUQUERQUE AIRPORT, C. 1950. Air travel also competed with Harvey Houses and trains. While Harvey ran the popular Kachina Room after 1948, it closed when a new airport opened in 1965. Even Harvey Girl requirements had changed. A 1945 ad in the *Albuquerque Journal* read: "Waitresses, Cafeteria and Lunch Room Women. Age 18 to 65. . . . Apply [at the] Alvarado Hotel." (Courtesy of Northern Arizona University, Cline Library, NAU.PH.95.44.112.)

A SANTA FE DINING CAR AND NATIVE AMERICAN GUIDES, C. 1950. In another ironic twist, Harvey Houses in the Southwest lost customers to the very trains that had brought travelers to Harvey House doors for decades. The Santa Fe Railway began to offer faster, more modern diesel-fueled trains that required far fewer time-consuming stops than the old steam engine trains. Air-conditioned dining and Pullman cars on trains with such romantic names as the *Super Chief* and the *Grand Canyon Limited* largely replaced Harvey House restaurant and hotel accommodations. By 1938, even those traveling on limited budgets during the Great Depression could ride *El Capitan*, with its well-advertised low-cost fares and meals. Native American guides were now hired to ride passenger trains and describe the landscape and Native American cultures to inquisitive travelers as their tourist trains sped through the Southwest. (Courtesy of Paul Nickens.)

SAILORS, SOLDIERS, AND CIVILIANS OUTSIDE THE ALVARADO, C. 1943. World War II suddenly reversed the downward spiral of Harvey House business. Harvey services were suddenly needed to feed tens of thousands of troops and civilians on the move across the country. Harvey Houses in Las Vegas, Albuquerque, Winslow, Needles, and Barstow became major troop train meal stops; tables were placed in every available space, from hallways to patios. With coffee and other food items rationed, menus (like the one with Navy insigne at left) stated that "coffee [is] limited to one cup per person." The company also established sandwich assembly lines at Harvey Houses in Albuquerque, Clovis, Gallup, and Williams. Harvey staff and local volunteers made as many as 3,500 sandwiches a day to feed troops whose trains lacked time to stop for meals. (Courtesy of the Albuquerque Museum, No. 1982.180.226.)

THE ALVARADO, 1943. Harvey House hotels were booked to capacity during World War II. With a severe housing shortage in Albuquerque, military families often stayed at the Alvarado until other facilities became available. El Tovar became a favorite destination for soldiers on furlough from Army installations in Arizona. In one instance, three Army airmen flying from Nevada to southern Arizona parachuted into the Grand Canyon when their B-24 developed engine trouble in mid-1944. Rescued, the three were brought to El Tovar shortly after their ordeal had ended. The old Harvey House in Kingman was used as temporary headquarters during the construction of the Kingman Army Airfield in 1942. The building was later used to house soldiers from the crowded airfield and to serve as a USO center. Harvey House personnel were even recruited to help in wartime surveillance. Just miles from the secret atomic research lab at Los Alamos, desk clerks and bar waiters at La Fonda were asked to listen for suspicious conversations; some claim that these clerks and waiters were, in fact, FBI agents. (Courtesy of Nancy Tucker.)

THE HARVEY GIRLS, 1946. As World War II drew to a successful close, Harvey Girls and the houses they served were celebrated in a major motion picture starring Judy Garland (as a novice Harvey Girl sent to a small New Mexico railroad town) and Angela Lansbury (as a dance hall queen), with a cameo appearance by Fred Harvey's grandson. Although its reviews were mixed (one reviewer called it "pure war-years escapism"), the movie's show-stopping song, "On the Atchison, Topeka, & Santa Fe," won an Oscar for the best movie song of 1946. In a fitting bow to a bygone era, the movie and its famous song helped to establish the Harvey Girls as true icons of American history and culture. (Courtesy of Marshall Trimble and the Belen Harvey House Museum.)

CLOSED SIGN AT THE ALVARADO, 1970. Despite their contributions to World War II and the popularity of *The Harvey Girls* film and hit song, Harvey Houses in the Southwest continued their steady decline in the postwar era, from 1945 to 1970. As before the war, modern transportation in the form of cars, buses, planes, and super trains had left the Harvey Houses as little more than anachronisms on the American landscape. Shortly after World War II, Harvey and Santa Fe officials toured the Southwest in a private train to inspect each Harvey House and determine its fate. As a result, three more Harvey Houses were closed, at La Junta, Las Vegas, and Needles. Seven more, at Ash Fork, Barstow, Clovis, Gallup, San Bernardino, Williams, and Winslow, joined the ill-fated houses in the 1950s. Albuquerque's Alvarado closed on January 2, 1970. (Courtesy of the Center for Southwest Research, University of New Mexico, No. 2000-014-0006.)

THE ALVARADO, FEBRUARY 1970. While the Santa Fe closed many Harvey Houses, the railroad went so far as to demolish 12 of its 26 Harvey structures in the Southwest, including those at Trinidad (1935), Lamy (1943), Kingman (1952), La Junta (1954), Gallup (1957), Ash Fork (1968), Albuquerque (1970), and, most recently, Seligman (2008); Colorado Springs, Raton, Rincon, and Vaughn were also razed, although the dates of their destruction are less clear. Great efforts were made to "stay" these "executions." In Albuquerque, alternative uses were proposed and protests were staged, but nothing could save the Alvarado after years of decline. A final Montezuma Ball was held on September 6, 1969, giving local residents a chance to bid farewell to a major part of their community and their lives. The Alvarado's furnishings were auctioned over several days. When Mary Colter heard of a similar auction held in 1959 to sell the furnishings she had used to decorate La Posada, she reportedly said, "Now I know there is such a thing as living too long." (Courtesy of the Museum of New Mexico, Photo Archives, No. 58706.)

NOT ALL HARVEY HOUSES FELL VICTIM TO THE WRECKING BALL. Several have been rescued to be used for new purposes, thanks to the Herculean efforts of local community leaders. As cultural landmarks, many houses are listed on state and national registers of historic places. After serving as a Baptist college (1922–1930) and as a Catholic seminary (1937–1972, above), the Montezuma has been renovated on the beautiful United World College campus. La Castañeda has served as apartments, a lounge, and the set of motion pictures, including Patrick Swayze's *Red Dawn* (1984). The Harvey House in Barstow is used as the town's railroad museum and city hall. The Harvey House in Clovis is used for railroad offices. The Belen Harvey House (below) served as sleeping quarters for railroad workers before becoming a popular Harvey House museum, attracting over 650 visitors a month.

ALBUQUERQUE TRANSPORTATION CENTER, 2008. After its old location lay vacant for over 30 years, the Alvarado has been replaced by a modern transportation center, designed with California Mission architecture remarkably similar to the old hotel's design. The Grand Canyon Railway Hotel, designed much like the Fray Marcos, opened in Williams in 1995; the old hotel now serves as a depot, curio shop, and museum. In 1997, Allan Affeldt and his artist wife, Tina Mion, purchased and remodeled La Posada (below), rehabilitating it to its former glory as one of Arizona's premier hotels; they have similar plans for El Graces in Needles. Great efforts have been made to rescue the still-standing, but threatened, Harvey House in Clovis. Finally, much of the Harvey Company's valuable art collection has been preserved in museums, especially the Heard Museum in Phoenix as of 1978.

EL TOVAR AND LA FONDA TODAY. In addition to La Posada, three other former Harvey establishments remain open as hotels. All are in private hands. La Fonda was sold to Sam Ballen in 1968, while El Tovar and Bright Angel were sold (along with the Harvey name and image) to the Amfac Corporation (now Xanterra Parks and Resorts) that same year. (The Santa Fe's passenger service became part of the Amtrak system in 1971.) Although remodeled several times, La Fonda, La Posada, El Tovar, and Bright Angel remain faithful to their original designs and are still rated among the top resorts of the Southwest. Fred Harvey would have been justly pleased that so much of his legendary hospitality survives not only in the memory of Southwestern history, but most importantly, in the service of modern travelers.

Visit us at
arcadiapublishing.com

CPSIA information can be obtained
at www.ICGtesting.com
Printed in the USA
LVHW101345230519
618878LV00023B/426/P